PRAISE FOR
THE 4 FORCES OF GROWTH

"This book doesn't just teach you how to grow your business—it teaches you how to grow yourself as a leader. Every CEO should keep a copy within arm's reach."

—Dr. Marshall Goldsmith, Thinkers50 #1 Executive Coach and *New York Times* bestselling author of *The Earned Life*, *Triggers*, and *What Got You Here Won't Get You There*

"Kevin's latest book is an MBA 'field manual' for experienced entrepreneurs who struggle to achieve growth. Kevin's '4 Forces of Growth' are not just explained but include real life examples that show how to implement each resource. Based on Kevin's thirty years of experience, the book challenges CEOs to honestly analyze their leadership assumptions and set goals to improve so they can achieve more of that elusive growth."

—Dr. Brad Smart, CEO of Topgrading, Inc.

"Kevin Lawrence's 4 Forces of Growth framework has given us the discipline to rise above daily distractions and channel our energy into what matters most for the business. That disciplined focus has not only fueled our growth but has also instilled confidence in our ability to scale with purpose and resilience for the long term."

—Andrew Limouris, founder, president, and CEO of Medix

"Growth is the hardest thing to teach a company, and it is the hardest DNA to find when hiring individuals. Every business and person thinks about growth differently. Kevin has found the right mix of examples, scientific data, and analogies from his studies to help readers drive growth both in themselves and their companies. *The 4 Forces of Growth* is a must-read for anyone looking to unleash growth. This book provides examples and charts helping paint the picture and a road map with specific ideas that will unlock the growth formula!"

—Brent Parent, CEO of TFS Global

"Kevin Lawrence is the rare coach who can simplify the complexity of business growth. His 4 Forces framework cuts through the noise and shows leaders where to concentrate and prioritize."

—Vishal, Ankur, and Varun Gupta, directors of Ashiana Housing Ltd.

"Kevin has a gift for seeing what happens behind closed doors when most leaders are their most vulnerable. He has been trusted with those moments, and in this book, he shares insights with honesty and wisdom. The result is a clear framework and a reflection of the struggles and breakthroughs every leader faces."

—Angela Santiago, CEO and cofounder of the Little Potato Company

"*The 4 Forces of Growth* masterfully focuses our attention on the criticality of prioritizing how we spend that most valuable of resources: our time. It is a must-read for any business leader serious about achieving *sustainable* growth."

—Mark Anderegg, professor of entrepreneurship at the Tuck School of Business at Dartmouth

"This book is a wake-up call for owner-led CEOs: Improving your business isn't the same as growing it. Kevin's 4 Forces framework shows you how to break through plateaus and reorient your energy toward sustainable, compounding growth."

—Brad Giles, founder of Evolution Partners and author of *Made to Thrive*, *Onboarded*, and *Bigger isn't Better, Better is Better*

"*The 4 Forces of Growth* gives CEOs a clear and practical road map to help themselves and their teams stay focused on what matters most for growth."

—Nancy MacKay, PhD, founder and CEO of MacKay CEO Forums

"When it comes to growing a company, it is rare to find an expert who can deliver the perfect balance of inspiration, intelligence, and instruction. Kevin delivers all three here. I highly recommend this book!"

—Mike Maddock, entrepreneur, author, and speaker

"Builders win with discipline: 90 percent A-players, Three Big Moves, and a CEO who stays on the strategic bike. Kevin Lawrence's *The 4 Forces of Growth* shows you how—so you can deliver superior results and an enduring legacy."

—Anthony Broccolini, CEO of Broccolini

"Kevin Lawrence excels at keeping the complexity of business growth simple. His 4 Forces framework cuts through the noise and shows CEOs and leaders exactly what matters most—and how to do it. You are provided a clear path to achieving real, consistent, and scalable growth by harnessing a few simple tools and avoiding common pitfalls."

—Tom King, executive partner, board of directors, Strategic Advisory LLC

"Lawrence has done it again! *Your Oxygen Mask First* has been my go-to business book, and now I have another in *The 4 Forces of Growth*! Kevin's 4 Forces framework has been a clarifying guide through T&T's rapid growth. It helps me stay focused on what's important when I find myself disoriented with all the competing priorities."

—Tina Lee, CEO of T&T Supermarket

"Kevin Lawrence's 4 Forces framework gives leaders the clarity and tools to focus on what matters most, execute with confidence, and achieve real, measurable growth."

—Kevin Brady, cofounder of Newbury Franklin

"The principles of this book work; I know because my organization is living it. Kevin was instrumental in catalyzing growth in me and the nonprofit I lead, using many of the tools found in *The 4 Forces of Growth*. Read the book, apply the lessons, and enjoy the ride."

—Dean Kurpjuweit, president of Union Gospel Mission

"Kevin has been our coach since 2018, guiding our team through leadership, mental health, and business strategy with clarity and care. His first book, *Your Oxygen Mask First*, became a foundational resource for us, and now *The 4 Forces of Growth* arrives at the perfect time. It is grounded in real-world experience, backed by thoughtful research, and written with remarkable precision. Kevin's ability to simplify complex ideas into actionable strategies makes this book a must-read for any team looking to grow with purpose. Thank you, Kevin, for continuing to inspire and elevate us."

—Kirk Fisher, P.Eng., MBA, CEO of Lark Group

"This book speaks to me! I've built a successful business over thirty-two years in the Middle East, and I wonder how much faster things could have been if I'd had the Growth Scientists' approach. The stories and tools resonated with me—I could clearly visualize the times I've been stuck on improvements or caught in the agony cycle of solving everyone's problems. As a CEO, you feel like you're being helpful—unsticking issues, making progress, even ticking off tasks—but you aren't moving the needle fast enough on growth. When I have been in harmony with growth, it's been when the leadership team is packed with A-Players and the momentum lifts the whole company."

—Hazel Jackson, CEO of Biz Group

"Reading *The 4 Forces of Growth* gave me an ah-ha moment as a CEO. It crystallized the role I need to play in driving growth and creating opportunity. Kevin's framework helped me step back, take full ownership of where our company is headed, and see growth not as a reactive outcome but as a responsibility. This book is both grounding and empowering. A must-read for any CEO ready to lead with purpose and clarity."

—Clara Jina Kim, cofounder and CEO of Cloré Beauty Supply

"Kevin brought a reassuring simplicity to one of the most complex journeys I have ever taken—the transformation to a CEO. Growth in a company isn't guaranteed but the way to drive growth in any company is mapped out succinctly in this book."

—David Porte, president of Porte Communities

"Kevin has once again delivered a masterpiece for CEOs and leaders. After teaching us to 'put on our oxygen mask first,' he now shows us how to harness 'the 4 Forces of Growth' to build companies that not only scale but thrive. What I admire most about this book is its blend of clarity and practicality—Kevin turns the chaos of growth into a road map any leader can follow. This is not theory, it's wisdom forged in the trenches with hundreds of growth-minded companies. Every CEO who wants to defy the odds and sustain growth should keep this book within reach."

—Cléo Maheux, founder of Hypergrowth

"Reading *The 4 Forces of Growth* was like turning on a light in a room I didn't realize was dim. Kevin's framework gave me clarity on the invisible dynamics that drive growth and, more importantly, how to harness them as a leader. This book is pragmatic, insightful, and packed with hard-won lessons from the trenches of scaling businesses. It's a must-read for any CEO who's serious about building something extraordinary."

—Clemens Kim, cofounder and president of Cloré Beauty Supply

"Kevin draws on over thirty years of experience coaching growth company leaders to deliver 130 pages of practical, no-nonsense insights. Like Kevin, it's direct, authentic, and focused on what works. If you're building or leading a growth company, read it—and more importantly, use it."

—Rick Holbrook, president and owner of Growth Stratagems

"We've known Kevin for over two decades. His gifts are to cut through the noise and make the complex simple, and his book is no different. His 4 Forces framework shows you exactly what to focus on to grow your company without losing your mind, your team, or your values."

—Isabelle Mercier and Margarita Romano,
cofounders of LeapZone Strategies

"Starting a business is hard. Scaling it is even harder. This book is your field manual to growing profitably—part wisdom, part strategy, and part tactical execution."

—Barry Moltz, M&A advisor and small business expert

THE 4 FORCES OF
GROWTH

THE 4 FORCES OF
GROWTH

Defy the Odds
and Keep Your
Company Scaling

KEVIN N. LAWRENCE

L&Co

Published by L&Co, Vancouver, BC
4forcesofgrowth.com
lawrenceandco.com

Edited and designed by Girl Friday Productions
www.girlfridayproductions.com

Cover design: Emily Weigel
Interior design: Rachel Marek
Project management: Emilie Sandoz-Voyer
Image credits: Graphics provided by Lawrence & Co

ISBN (hardcover): 978-1-0696700-0-7
ISBN (paperback): 978-1-0696700-1-4
ISBN (ebook): 978-1-0696700-2-1

First edition

I dedicate this book to the bold leaders who pour their hearts and minds into building companies that transform our world. I recognize your bravery to embrace the personal growth the journey demands. May your own evolution mirror the positive change you seek to create.

CONTENTS

INTRODUCTION

Greatness, it turns out, is largely a matter
of conscious choice and discipline.

—Jim Collins

The Obsession with Growth

I'm sitting here in Thailand—Phuket, to be precise—thinking about business growth and my obsession with it. Since you're reading this book, I'm willing to bet you're obsessed with it too.

You and I both know the drive to grow a company is not simply about accumulating wealth. Shareholder value, ROI, and revenue growth are merely scorecards for success. The bigger game is inward. It's a personal quest for fulfillment and excellence. It's the drive to make a difference for your family, your community, and the world. It's creating something and seeing how far you can take it.

In my mind, growing a business is akin to magic. You're manifesting on a rare level, conjuring something out of nothing.

No matter what stage of growth you are in right now—whether you're at the earliest or most advanced stages—you're doing something that takes creativity, relentless execution, and a level of self-belief few mortals possess.

The Hustle Begins

I didn't start out in life hobnobbing with CEOs or knowing anything about the business world. Far from it. I was a scrappy kid from North Delta, British Columbia (just outside of Vancouver), hustling to make my way in the world. But from the get-go, I always loved a challenge.

I've constantly pushed myself to conquer fears and acquire competencies—often several at the same time. Like public speaking, where I went from terrified to thrilled, I now address huge audiences. The need for speed? I channelled it to become a skilled race car driver. Inner calm? I learned to tame my busy mind (at times), a feat I once thought impossible.

For me, every new challenge is a chance to stretch my limits. When I master something, I'm restless until I choose the next thing. Let me guess . . . this sounds familiar to you, doesn't it?

We growth seekers have a lot in common. We want to achieve the extraordinary.

No matter what stage of growth you are in right now—whether you're at the earliest or most advanced stages—you're doing something that takes creativity, relentless execution, and a level of self-belief few mortals possess.

From Lawns to Laundry

Picture this: It's my second year of college, and I'm juggling a full course load while running the landscaping business I founded to pay for school. Every morning, I'd meet my crew at six thirty, get them started on the day's jobs, then rush to campus for classes.

One day, as I burst into the lecture hall, frazzled and running late from my crew meeting, I heard a voice say, "There he is!" and to my horror, a lecture hall of two hundred students turned to stare at me.

I sheepishly walked into the room, certain I was about to be reprimanded by the dean peering up from the lectern. But instead, I was met with thunderous applause. I was receiving my program's most prestigious award for academics and community service, landing me a series of internships across Vancouver.

Thanks to one of those internships, I landed a job in the media business, where I eventually met my very first client, Steve Majewski. I pitched Steve on letting me market his mobile dry cleaning business called Wheely Clean. And with that, my journey as a growth consultant was born, though I didn't know it at the time. What I did know was that business was a way to push myself and evolve my life. And like I said, I always love a challenge.

The Growth Conundrum

It started slow, but after a few years, my little consulting business started thriving far beyond what I imagined—first locally, then through Canada and the United States. Eventually I found myself working with remarkable CEOs around the world. I was simultaneously an advisor to these great leaders and an observer, soaking up lessons just from being in their presence.

Through these observations, a grand and baffling conundrum emerged. I sometimes saw brilliant CEOs with years of success take unnecessary tumbles, some even bringing their companies right to the ground. I remember one CEO whose company went from being a tech industry darling to disappearing into obscurity, with products still light years beyond the market.

Another CEO built a business worth hundreds of millions of dollars, only to be forced into a fire sale after a disastrous financial decision. Another carved out a new product category, grew sizably, only to lose everything to a small competitor just when the market was really taking off.

To me, none of this made sense. How can amazing companies with sharp CEOs and tons of opportunity simply stop growing or collapse altogether?

Some CEOs always seemed to be able to stay the course and pivot as needed, while others—just as smart—were dragged into mediocrity or oblivion.

Initially I wondered, Do some CEOs simply lose the will to grow? Or do these accomplished leaders feel they've already achieved enough?

In almost every case, the answers were decidedly no. These leaders absolutely aspired to keep growing. They still had the internal drive to build and create.

> **We growth seekers have a lot in common. We want to achieve the extraordinary.**

I knew something else was going on. There had to be hidden forces at play, mysterious elements so powerful they could derail even the most seasoned leaders.

And with that, the central challenge of my career was born. For thirty years, I've been unravelling the greatest mystery of business: *Why is it so ridiculously hard to keep a great company growing?*

The Growth Scientist

With this puzzle in mind, I became what you could call a Growth Scientist.

For three decades, I've worked side by side with CEOs and their leadership teams, rigorously testing every growth theory, methodology, and framework I could get my hands on. I have delved into models, tools, research findings, and new and old management philosophies. I've left no stone unturned in my quest.

Time and again, I've found that the simplest things always work best. That's not to say growth is easy, but rather it's more straightforward than you might imagine.

I've been part of strategies that generated billions in revenue, and I've played my part in about $350 million worth of missteps. This wealth of experience spans an array of sectors across North America, the Middle East, Asia, Australia, and Europe.

I now have a team of growth advisors working with more than one hundred mid-market companies, comprising thousands of employees and backed by billions of dollars.

We don't swoop in for a whirlwind strategy session and disappear. We're deeply embedded with these companies. We conduct hands-on growth experiments quarter after quarter, year after year, meticulously tracking results, refining strategies, and scrapping what doesn't work. We take growth theory to growth science.

Our approach allows us to see beyond short-term fluctuations and truly understand what generates long-term growth.

> **Time and again, I've found that the simplest things always work best. That's not to say growth is easy, but rather it's more straightforward than you might imagine.**

Now, against all odds, this scrappy kid from North Delta regularly finds himself conversing with extraordinary CEOs, helping them diagnose their growth problems and capture their growth opportunities. I could not be more astonished or delighted by this turn of events.

Remarkable Leaders, Remarkable Results

The proof of the approach we take at my company, Lawrence & Co, is best illustrated through the leaders we work with. Their stories of transformation and growth are testaments to what's possible when time-tested growth science meets visionary leadership and hard work.

In India, the Gupta brothers—Vishal, Ankur, and Varun—transformed Ashiana, their father's homebuilding business. They're now constructing and selling thousands of homes across the country annually. They describe their purpose as "nurturing smiles" by creating vibrant communities for families and seniors.

Meanwhile, Tina Lee is revolutionizing the grocery landscape. She took T&T Supermarkets, the grocery business her mother founded in Vancouver, and expanded it to more than forty supermarkets—making it Canada's largest Asian grocery chain. Under Tina's dynamic leadership, T&T has become a go-to national brand, a cornerstone of the Asian Canadian community, and a new entry into the US market. She isn't just selling products—she's bridging cultures.

Then there's John McLean and his family, who own Bundaberg Brewed Drinks in Australia, crafting what many consider the best ginger beer in the world. They took a family recipe made with real ginger and turned it into a worldwide sensation exporting to sixty-one countries. Their range of brewed non-alcoholic beverages are made with real ingredients, and each flavour has been crafted to treat the world to Bundaberg.

Ben Godsey has redefined what it means to support local businesses. He transformed ProService Hawaii from a small, local provider of outsourced HR services into a dynamic force serving more than 90,000 employees across Hawaii and the US mainland. Over the past two decades, ProService has grown from a single office in Kailua-Kona to Hawaii's most successful growth company. It has achieved 18 percent annualized organic growth for more than twenty years and has been a Hawaii's Best Places to Work award winner for eighteen years running.

Andrew Limouris, the son of Greek immigrants, turned Medix Staffing Solutions into a healthcare and life sciences staffing giant approaching $500 million in revenue. Andrew and his team aren't just filling thousands of medical jobs across North America every week; they're on a mission to positively impact lives. He wrote about this in his book *Won with Purpose.*

These leaders, each with their unique stories, share a common thread—a commitment to keep growing. Their successes extend beyond numbers on income statements or balance sheets. They're fuelled by purpose: to create lasting good for customers, employees, communities, and the broader economy.

I share more stories throughout this book, and sometimes I've changed names and identifying details. When a name is changed you'll see an asterisk (*) to note that. Most of these companies have achieved at least $100 million in revenue. Some have reached a billion or more.

Your Invitation to Warp-Speed Learning

Usually CEOs who achieve long-term growth do so by earning a PhD or two from the School of Hard Knocks. After a series of heartaches, setbacks, and heroic turnarounds, they come out the other side knowing how to keep a company growing.

I'd like to make your learning curve faster and easier. I aim to share the lessons I've learned from decades in the field, in the most concise, straightforward way possible. As I've explained, this book isn't armchair theory. It's the distillation of three decades of rigorous testing and hard-won experience.

It reveals the few essential principles that create significant, long-term growth. Consider this a Growth Scientist's playbook, written specifically for leaders like you.

My goal is to help you grow your company to ten times its size and realize your most audacious ambitions. Whether you're aiming to scale from tens of millions to hundreds of millions in revenue, or from hundreds of millions to billions, the principles in this book can guide you.

Of course, I can't prevent your heartaches or setbacks entirely. Those are ultimately part of business and life. But I can share crucial lessons on running your business in a way that makes mistakes and obstacles more survivable, helping you stay on the path of growth no matter what.

Let's Define Growth

Before we go further, let's define what I mean when I talk about growth.

You've likely heard the saying "Revenue is vanity, profit is sanity, and cash is king." It's a popular saying in business circles for good reason. Some organizations become so fixated on revenue, they neglect profit and cash flow, leading to precarious situations. I wholeheartedly agree that you can't run a business focused on revenue alone.

But when I see great companies lose their grip on growth, they've often got profit and cash well managed, but they're not paying close enough attention to a metric I call Real Growth.

Real Growth: The Heart of This Book

Real Growth is increasing the number of X's (or units) you sell, with the assumption you're at least sustaining, and ideally increasing, your profit per X.

Your X depends on your unique situation. It might be transactions, subscriptions, memberships, billable hours, or customer visits—you get the idea.

When you're increasing your X's, you're selling more square footage, subscriptions, memberships, or whatever your X is. When you're increasing your profit per X, you're making more on each one you sell.

I'd like to give credit to Jim Collins, who popularized the use of profit per X with his book *Good to Great*.

Why Not Profit Alone?

You may wonder, Why not only focus on profit? As companies grow, they often become more focused on efficiency and profitability (profit per X) at the expense of selling more X's.

Profit is baked into accounting models, financial reporting, executive incentives, and other standard business practices. CFOs and their teams often vigilantly monitor margins. When profit needs attention, they make sure it happens.

That's why this book assumes your organization already has healthy discipline concerning profit. If you need guidance, however, there are countless books available, including the cash chapter in *Scaling Up*—a book for which I was a key contributor. (See the Resources section at the end of this book.)

But it's crucial to remember that you can have an incredibly profitable company that never actually grows. This book tackles that challenge, helping you ensure your company continues to sell more X's over the long haul. In my view, this is the simplest, yet most overlooked, aspect of growing a business.

> **It's crucial to remember that you can have an incredibly profitable company that never actually grows. This book tackles that challenge.**

Now, it needs to be said that companies naturally cycle through periods when they need to improve profit. So, of course, be attuned to this. But always be aware, profit is only part of the story, and profit alone won't get you where you want to go.

Why Not Revenue Growth or Enterprise Value?

You might also wonder why I don't simply use revenue growth as the metric. While it's a common measure of growth, it can be misleading. You can increase revenue by raising prices but sell fewer X's, meaning your company can be in decline despite improving revenues.

As for enterprise value, it can be affected by market conditions, investor sentiment, and other external factors that don't necessarily reflect the actual growth of your business operations.

The Real Growth Mantra: Sell More X's

To recap, Real Growth is created by selling more X's and at least sustaining your profit per X.

This book focuses predominantly on the challenge of selling more X's—an obstacle that can derail even the most remarkable companies.

With that, let's proceed.

PART 1

Understanding Growth

CHAPTER 1

Why Is It So Hard to Keep a Great Company Growing?

The successful warrior is the average person with laser-like focus.

—Bruce Lee

If you're like most CEOs I know, you are inherently wired for growth. Maybe you've expanded a business regionally or across borders. Maybe you've grown several companies from scratch. Whatever your situation, you wouldn't be where you are without years of proven growth and a certain amount of business acumen running through your veins.

And like most CEOs I've met, you've probably devised your own personal approach for growing a business that's worked for years. You've got a nose for opportunity. You've got an instinct and skill for problem-solving and for making sure customers and employees are heard and cared for.

When everything is humming, you probably feel unstoppable. But in my experience, even the most remarkable CEOs in the world, almost without exception, can all get stuck and lose their grip on growth.

At first glance, the reasons for this are mysterious. Savvy, proven CEOs suddenly start making flawed decisions. Despite a fierce commitment to growth, they may fail to make a much-needed and obvious market pivot. They may find themselves in a dangerous cash crunch for no good reason. Or another strange and disastrous situation occurs, and growth grinds to a halt. I've seen far too many great CEOs forced to dilute their ownership or flat out sell their companies in these situations.

I can tell you from close observation, in most cases, this isn't a lack of genius, drive, or market opportunity. Most CEOs I've observed have all three in spades. So what is it?

Big Circle, Little Circle

My first insight into this odd phenomenon came from a man in Toledo. Brent "BP" Parent is the CEO of Total Fleet Solutions, a company with expertise in all areas of material handling. My first assignment with BP was to create a post-acquisition vision and strategy.

BP is like many great CEOs I've known—down-to-earth, unassuming, curious, and driven. In my initial meetings with him and his executive team, he didn't say much, preferring to listen intently to the other leaders.

When everything is humming, you probably feel unstoppable. But in my experience, even the most remarkable CEOs in the world, almost without exception, can all get stuck and lose their grip on growth.

But at one point, deep into a strategy conversation, one of his executives, Tommy, raised a nightmare operational issue for the group to discuss. And out of the blue, quiet BP spoke up: "Tommy, are you in the big circle or the little circle?" The question was blunt but accompanied by a wide, knowing grin. The energy shifted in the room.

Confused, I switched my gaze to Tommy, who now had a knowing smile of his own. He sighed and cast his eyes downward.

I needed to know what in the world was going on, so I said, "What do you mean, big circle? Little circle?"

With that, BP stood up and drew two circles on a whiteboard. "Tommy, what's in the big circle?" he inquired.

"Opportunities," came the response.

BP: "And the little circle?"

Tommy: "Problems."

BP: "Right. And how much time do we spend in the big circle?"

Tommy: "Ninety-five percent."

BP: "And how much time in the little circle?"

Tommy: "Five percent."

BP: "Exactly. And if any of you need help with problems, come to my office in the morning between eight and eight thirty." With his Cheshire cat grin, he added, "I'll be there at nine. But if you've got an opportunity, call me any time of day."

From BP, I learned that a CEO's job is to maintain an unwavering focus on growth opportunities, address only crucial problems, and coach the senior leaders to do the same.

Know Where You're Headed

Another outstanding CEO I've learned from is Angela Santiago, cofounder and CEO of the Edmonton-based Little Potato Company. Angela has a knack for seeing around corners.

When her company hit $30 million, she knew she needed top-tier talent to keep growing. But there was a catch—she wanted a calibre of executive that was far beyond her means. Knowing she was navigating to a long-term goal of $1 billion in revenue, she wanted big league players.

So when the time came to hire a new sales executive, Angela made an unconventional move. She approached a hotshot leader with experience running $500 million sales operations and convinced him to join her team two days a week.

Her peers thought she was crazy. "Why pay so much for part-time help?" they asked. But Angela's response was simple: "I'd rather have world-class talent part-time than typical talent full-time."

The gamble paid off. Within months, the new sales leader had increased revenue substantially. Quarter after quarter, he kept landing giant deals, and the business eventually grew enough for Angela to hire him full-time. This became her signature move—hiring beyond the company's size as a means to accelerate growth.

"Most CEOs play it safe, hiring for where they are now," Angela told me. "But if you want exponential growth, you need to hire for where you're going."

Now, after many years of expansion, the company is thriving in Canada and the United States and is on the lookout for new markets.

From Angela, I learned about courage. I learned about keeping your eyes to the sky, never flinching from your long-term vision.

An Unrelenting Focus on Growth

BP and Angela are rare exceptions. They constantly remember to focus on growth no matter how noisy and complicated life becomes. No matter what direction other people want to pull them. And no matter what may seem impossible right now.

This may sound obvious. But with the constant demands, distractions, and competing priorities of running a growing business, it's extraordinarily hard to stay focused on Real Growth. You're battling day-to-day urgencies and intense opinions and emotions from team members and customers. Your brain wants to pay attention to all of it. It wants to address all of it. It wants to worry about all of it.

> **Growth is inherently messy, creating noise that can easily distract leaders from their ultimate intentions.**

But to keep growing, leaders need to remember that Real Growth is selling more X's. They need to stay focused on this even when it seems like they should deprioritize it. Even when it seems impossible to focus on it. This ability, in my experience, is what separates the companies that keep growing from those that don't.

The Growth Killers

Contrary to what many people believe, it's rarely a lack of opportunity that stops a company from growing. The real culprits? The distractions of problems and fear. These are the true growth killers.

Growth is inherently messy, creating noise that can easily distract leaders from their ultimate intentions. The most successful CEOs carefully navigate this chaos, maintaining their focus on growth—no matter what.

Other CEOs, who may have kept these forces at bay for years, can suddenly find themselves sucked into a vortex of problems or fear, causing growth to slide.

This usually happens in one of two ways:

1. **The company gets lost in problems.** Leaders and employees become overly focused on fixing issues and making improvements rather than driving Real Growth. This happens when people fail to filter and prioritize effectively, addressing fifty-cent problems instead of $5 million opportunities. They become intoxicated by improvements and seduced by streamlining.

2. **The company gets bogged down by fear.** Decision-making becomes paralyzed as everyone

spends time, energy, and money analyzing options to avoid a misstep. Leaders shift from a mindset of trying, testing, and learning to one of seeking to avoid failure. They move from playing to win to playing not to lose.

In a Nutshell

Most CEOs struggle with growth not because they lack opportunity or ambition, but because they become distracted by problems or paralyzed by fear.

- To maintain Real Growth (increasing your X's while sustaining or increasing your profit per X), you must consciously resist the gravitational pull of problems while carefully managing fear.
- Remember, making your business better isn't the same as making it bigger—you can't improve your way to growth.
- Spend 95 percent of your time on opportunities and 5 percent on problems.

Questions

What percent of your time do you spend on opportunities versus problems?

_____

_____

_____

_____

_____

_____

_____

_____

_____

_____

What would be ideal for you?

_____

_____

_____

_____

_____

_____

_____

_____

_____

_____

_____

_____

CHAPTER 2

Spatial Disorientation

Your eyes can deceive you.
Don't trust them.

—Obi-Wan Kenobi

Pilots can lose all sense of orientation midair, not knowing what direction the plane is headed. They may believe it is on track when it's actually headed for a crash. This is called spatial disorientation.

Kim "KC" Campbell is an elite aviator who flew more than a hundred combat missions in Iraq and Afghanistan, eventually receiving the Distinguished Flying Cross for heroism.

She told me an incredible story of a night mission, 20,000 feet above Afghanistan. She had finished refuelling midair and was rolling away from the air tanker. It was a maneuver she'd performed countless times, but that night something was different.

The movement of the rolling plane shattered her perception of reality. Maybe it was the combination of the blackness of the night sky, the reflection of the tanker, and the narrow sightline of her night vision goggles, but suddenly she couldn't perceive which direction to go.

In that moment, KC's world spiralled into chaos. The tanker seemed to be everywhere at once, its lights reflecting off wispy clouds, creating a kaleidoscope of confusion. Her heart raced as she realized she had lost all sense of up and down, left and right.

The mountains below, shrouded in darkness, offered no reference point. With each passing second, the risk of a collision with the tanker or the unforgiving terrain below increased.

"It was terrifying—total sensory overload," she explained. "I had to will myself to trust my flight instruments."

KC fought against panic, forcing herself to focus on her instrument panel. With human lives and the success of the mission hanging in the balance, she battled the confusion that gripped her senses.

Deferring to her instruments, KC managed to right the plane, pull away from the tanker, and continue on with her mission. It was a stark reminder of the razor-thin line between life and death that fighter pilots face in every moment.

Skewed Perception

KC's harrowing experience in the skies of Afghanistan might seem far removed from the executive suite, but the parallels are striking. Just as pilots like KC can lose their bearings,

CEOs can get disoriented in the high-pressure dynamics of business growth.

Every day, you're navigating through market changes, competitive threats, the regulatory environment, and internal challenges. Along the way, problems and fear can cloud your vision, making it difficult to distinguish between what's truly important and what's not. This can cause you to focus on the wrong things and to inadvertently make choices that steer you away from growth. This is the executive's version of spatial disorientation, and it's what makes sustaining growth so challenging.

And much like a pilot, your stakes are incredibly high. Livelihoods depend on your decisions. The very existence of your company may be at risk.

Let me give you an example of how easy it is for leaders to become disoriented. A few summers ago, I met with a new client, *Luis, who asked me to uncover why his sales were lagging. Luis is in the manufacturing business, with a huge roster of customers, enviable margins, and a solid sales history. But something was amiss. He was losing grip on his ambitious long-range growth targets. The past two years had been disappointing financially, and no one in his business knew why.

As I chatted with Luis and his sharp leadership team, who had everything nailed down, their operational and technical prowess was clear as day. I was dazzled by stories of constant product evolution, lightning-fast service response times, and joyful customers. This team ran like a Swiss watch.

Impressed, I asked them to talk me through their strategy for the coming year. I was expertly guided through a series of impressive project plans. Each was rigorous, meticulous, and artfully explained. I heard about plans to add product features, create even quicker response times, and install a fancy new sales automation system. But not one single plan spoke to growth—selling more X's. Everything was about business improvement.

When I (gently) pointed this out to the team, they pushed back, emphatically defending the importance of their initiatives. But as we talked more, they gradually understood that they had become so engrossed with perfecting their products and systems, they had stopped focusing on growth. They were confusing improving the business with growing it.

If only I could shout this message loud enough that every CEO on the planet could hear it:

> *Improving a company is not the same as growing a company. Better isn't the same as bigger. You can have a beautifully managed business that never grows, and many CEOs do.*

Tweaking and refining your products and operations are worthy endeavours, but they rarely drive growth. Sure, there are rare situations when a product upgrade is so compelling customers line up in droves—but this is not the reality for most businesses.

Instead, improvements usually serve a different purpose: They keep existing customers happy and loyal. They boost profit per X, increase customer satisfaction, and strengthen your company's foundation. All vital goals, but distinct from growth itself.

Tweaking and refining your products and operations are worthy endeavours, but they rarely drive growth.

I worked with Luis and his team to shift their focus to include some significant growth initiatives. I felt their discomfort—expansion projects feel risky. They're not the sure-fire slam dunks of improvement initiatives. But with a genuine focus on new markets, new products, and new partnerships, lo and behold, the business started to grow again.

Luis's story demonstrates how intoxicating and disorienting problems can be. Fixing and improving the business feels useful. But when the end of the year rolls around, you may discover that although a lot happened, the business stood still.

Even the best leaders can fall prey to a distorted view of reality. You can believe you're navigating toward growth, making all the right moves, but your perspective can be dangerously off-kilter.

> **Improving a company is not the same as growing a company. Better isn't the same as bigger. You can have a beautifully managed business that never grows, and many CEOs do.**

In a Nutshell

Just as pilots can lose their bearings mid-flight, CEOs can become disoriented by the complexity and pressure of running a growing business. This can cause you to focus on the wrong priorities and inadvertently make choices that steer you away from growth.

- Without a definitive focus on selling more X's, it's easy to mistake business improvement for business growth.
- The key to avoiding disaster is maintaining a crystal-clear view of which initiatives truly drive Real Growth versus those that improve operations or mitigate risk.

Questions

What's the number one thing that drives Real Growth in your business?

_____

_____

_____

_____

_____

_____

_____

_____

_____

_____

What could you spend more or less time on to better lead Real Growth?

_____

_____

_____

_____

_____

_____

_____

_____

_____

_____

_____

CHAPTER 3

The Problem of Problems

Why do you stay in prison when
the door is so wide open?

—Rumi

About a decade ago, I was called in to help a Canadian CEO through a time of crisis. A master of sales and strategy, *Tara was accustomed to being out in the world, building relationships, and striking deals.

But her company was hit with a series of misfortunes. Two senior leaders left within months of each other. A key supplier went out of business. And the implementation of a new ERP system went sideways, throwing operations into a tailspin.

Like any great CEO, Tara shifted into crisis mode. She rolled up her sleeves and assumed the jobs of both departed executives, meaning she was now playing the roles of CFO and COO in addition to her own. She also stepped in to personally oversee the ERP project, dragging it back from the brink of disaster.

> **The magnetic pull of problems lurks in every growing business, and it's the single biggest reason CEOs stop focusing on growth.**

Day and night, Tara was in the office, spending hours upon hours in internal meetings, hammering out solutions to a cesspool of problems. After I supported her through a long and gruelling year, a calm set in. She'd hired an amazing CFO and COO. Her ERP system was humming. She'd replaced her old supplier with a new one and secured contracts with two backups.

But now, what started as a nightmare had become a way of life. Tara was so accustomed to being in the thick of day-to-day business, she was infuriating the new CFO and COO. She couldn't detach. She surprised herself at how much she enjoyed the frenzy and satisfaction of being in the trenches. This is the strange allure of problem-solving. It's intoxicating.

The magnetic pull of problems lurks in every growing business, and it's the single biggest reason CEOs stop focusing on growth. Let's dig into why.

The Perilous Line

Broadly speaking, business problems fall into two categories: fixing things and improving things. They masquerade as the most essential to-dos of running a business. That's what makes them dangerous.

There's a perilously fine line between prudent problem-solving and getting lost in a maze of issues. Problems have an insidious tendency to consume every ounce of your energy and resources, distracting you from growth.

Before we go further, it's important to understand that problems themselves aren't inherently bad. In fact, they serve a crucial function.

> **Think of problems as the warning lights on your car's dashboard.**

Problems are an alert system for your company. They point out where things are amiss, whether it's a broken process, an unmet customer expectation, or some other imbalance.

Think of problems as the warning lights on your car's dashboard. Some alert you to minor issues that can be addressed at your convenience—like a tire that's slightly underinflated. Others, like a flashing empty fuel or battery indicator, demand urgent attention.

The real challenge is discernment. As a leader, you need to develop the skill of quickly assessing which problems require immediate action and which don't—a task more difficult than it seems.

To understand how leaders like Tara get caught in this trap, you need to consider how problem-solving evolves as a company grows.

The Evolution Problem

When a company starts out, problems are straightforward. A big problem is obviously a big problem. A need for improvement is evident. And growth initiatives easily take centre stage simply because you're building your foundation.

Then the business expands and complexity creeps in. Now you're not only in building mode—you're also in operations mode. Service hiccups arise. Customers raise concerns. Systems break. So you add more people to help with all the growth and all the problems. They bring fresh ideas for improvement. And guess what else they bring? You got it. More problems.

Every member of your team believes their problem is mission critical. And as CEO, your job is to sort through everything, prioritize, and make sound decisions about where resources are invested and where they're not. All while you concentrate on increasing your X's, which generates more growth and—inevitably—more problems. Only now, the problems are even bigger, noisier, and more complicated.

> **Every member of your team believes their problem is mission critical. And as CEO, your job is to sort through everything, prioritize, and make sound decisions about where resources are invested and where they're not.**

Before you know it, you're no longer spending most of the week meeting with customers and partners, hiring great talent, and identifying new markets. You're no longer doing the core work to increase your X's. Instead you're in the trenches, knee-deep in technology issues and operational mishaps and jumping in to support underperforming team members.

This is how problems slowly hijack your focus. Too much attention on them pulls resources from growth activities. Not enough focus on them, and the wheels of the business start coming off.

The People Problem

Of all the problems CEOs face, people problems are the toughest to address. Yet they're also the ones leaders most regret not handling sooner.

I can't even count the number of times I've heard a leader say, "I've learned my lesson: Next time, I'll have the uncomfortable conversation immediately." Human nature gets in the way. For most, it never gets easier to have difficult conversations about underperformance, or a lack of fit, or any other type of interpersonal issue.

Case in point: One of my clients hired a new CFO for his fast-growing company. Within forty-one days, the CFO's behaviour created so much drama that the leadership team was barely recognizable. He was manipulating and scheming behind everyone's backs. The team went from lighthearted and collaborative to distrustful and angry. And I say this to you again: It all happened in only forty-one days.

I experienced the drama firsthand when the troublemaker targeted me in a quarterly planning session. This spurred the CEO and me into action. We quickly went into reconnaissance mode, and the next step became abundantly clear. He fired the disruptor on Day 42, but it took quite some time for the team to regain its stride.

The big lesson here: Don't wait to solve a people problem. Action must be swift and decisive.

> ## Of all the problems CEOs face, people problems are the toughest to address.

The Priority Problem

Beyond people problems, how do you know which issues truly deserve your attention? It comes down to brutal facts and basic math.

You must address any issue that, if left unchecked, could lead to catastrophic results. In his masterwork *Good to Great*, Jim Collins calls these "brutal facts." These are problems that could impact the safety of your employees, seriously impair your ability to deliver to clients, impede future growth, or threaten the very existence of your business.

The trouble is, some problems appear to be of this magnitude when they are not. You must do the math. Generally, hard numbers can tell you which problems could sink the ship and which are choppy waters you can navigate. Of course, the safety of human beings is always deemed priceless.

Remember Tara? I helped her reorient to growth mode. She had to let other people do their jobs and rediscover her first love—conquering market opportunities. She let go of leading operational and technology projects and turned her focus to the external world, building relationships with customers and partners.

Maybe you see yourself in Tara. I bet remarkable problem-solving skills are part of the reason you ended up as a CEO in the first place. And let's be honest—it feels great to be a hero. Customers rejoice. People shower you with praise. You go home at night feeling like you made a difference for someone—because you did.

But if a CEO is focused on problems, the rest of the team falls into the same trap, and the whole company ends up in firefighting mode.

In a Nutshell

There may be times of crisis when you need to be Chief Problem Solver temporarily. But no CEO or leadership team should always be in firefighting mode if growth is their goal.

- Remember that problems are warning signs that need to be assessed for severity or potential severity.
- Address the critical problems swiftly but never lose sight of the horizon. Don't let the allure of problem-solving distract you from your primary focus: increasing your X's.
- If you're stuck in firefighting mode, my book *Your Oxygen Mask First* is for you. Check out chapter 12, "Stop Being Chief Problem Solver."

Questions

What kinds of problems are you most easily distracted by?

_____

_____

_____

_____

_____

_____

_____

Which problems could deserve more attention?

_____

_____

_____

_____

_____

_____

_____

Less?

_____

_____

_____

_____

_____

_____

_____

CHAPTER 4

The Friction of Fear

The only limit to our realization of
tomorrow will be our doubts of today.

—Amelia Earhart

I live in Vancouver, British Columbia, and regularly drive the
Coquihalla Highway to the Okanagan Valley. It's one of North
America's most dangerous winter roads—so terrifying there's
even a TV series about it called *Highway Thru Hell*. Some lo-
cals refuse to drive it in winter, even though it leads to one of
the province's most desirable destinations.

Although I drive that highway regularly, I take every pre-
caution. I have a truck with the best studded snow tires, sand-
bags in the back for weight, and a safety kit. I'm aware of the

risks, and I'm prepared for them. But I don't let them keep me from a place I love.

This is what it's like to manage a growing company. You're venturing to a thrilling destination, and you need to be prudent. You need to be aware of the risks at every turn, carefully deciding which ones are worth taking and proceeding wisely.

The Analysis Trap

Since you're a leader, I already know you're a courageous person. Someone without courage would never take the top job, much less stay there for the long term. You know the thrill of signing off on a bold move and guiding a team to a major win.

But even the bravest leaders can fall into the analysis trap, where fear masquerades as diligence. Let me tell you about *Prishna.

Prishna leads a chic clothing brand with vast success across Asia and Australia. In the early years, she had one staggering success after another: celebrities wearing her fashions, industry awards, global press coverage, and sales that wouldn't quit. She had such a golden touch that she started to feel invincible.

Against the advice of some sage advisors, she decided she was ready to take on the US market. She hired a team of American executives and jumped in full force, opening several stores at once.

Within a year, her highly profitable brand-name business was on the verge of bankruptcy. She'd taken on too much too fast, overextending her ability to absorb mistakes and financial losses. She had no other choice but to shutter all her American locations and retreat back home to salvage the rest of her business.

When I met her, she was still fresh from this trauma and

trying to find a way forward. This once-vibrant CEO had become hesitant and small. Her executive team would present opportunities and ideas, and she would continually delay, always needing more time to weigh options. She requested more data, more market assessments, and more opinions. She was terrified of making another big mistake and losing everything.

> **Even the bravest leaders can fall into the analysis trap, where fear masquerades as diligence.**

In our work together, Prishna discovered that the antidote to analysis paralysis was to put numbers to her fears. She developed financial modelling to calculate realistic worst-case and best-case scenarios for her decisions. With a mathematical foundation for her choices, she could evaluate risks objectively and distinguish between those that could hurt her business and those that could destroy it.

The Burnout Spiral

Fear doesn't always shout. Sometimes it whispers through the hallways of success, disguised as exhaustion. This is what happened to *Dan.

Dan runs a structural engineering firm in London, providing services for commercial building projects across the United Kingdom and France. The twenty-five-year history of his business reads like a novel. He's been through everything imaginable: incredible triumphs, tough losses, personal struggles, betrayals by trusted partners, near bankruptcy, and then financial success well beyond his dreams.

When I met him, he wanted help jump-starting a niche vertical for testing and compliance. He hoped an outside eye would clarify the best steps forward and invigorate his team.

But in his meetings with me, he was lukewarm in his commitment to the opportunity. His logic was blurry and his enthusiasm tepid. I heard excuse after excuse about what might go wrong. I'm a bundle of energy, but I'd leave those meetings feeling lethargic.

Dan's version of fear was burnout—a state where decision-making becomes slow and arduous, courage evaporates, and it's nearly impossible to think clearly or move forward with anything. Leaders like Dan are the reason I wrote the book *Your Oxygen Mask First* to help executives personally recharge and keep going.

While I worked with him, it became clear that his burnout was more than personal exhaustion alone—it was a symptom of a deeper organizational issue. His leadership team wasn't strong enough to support him through the challenges and opportunities he faced. His team excelled at managing long-standing projects and clients but not launching brand initiatives.

> **Fear doesn't always shout.**
> **Sometimes it whispers through**
> **the hallways of success,**
> **disguised as exhaustion.**

My team and I addressed Dan's personal resilience head-on, working with him to rebuild his energy and establish practices to keep him thriving. He found ways to prioritize his mental health and overall well-being. Now he meditates daily and works out three times a week without fail. He picked up his guitar again after twenty years and rediscovered his love of music.

We strengthened his leadership team, replacing a few key positions with people who had the know-how to drive the business forward. It took some time, but Dan found himself reinvigorated and reoriented toward growth. He was once again able to make courageous decisions with certainty and enthusiasm.

In fact, he boldly passed on his original project in favour of a partnership that truly excited him. He signed a deal with a major European engineering group, allowing him to quickly expand into five new countries. His revenue doubled in four years.

Fear Is Your Friend

Fear isn't your enemy—it's actually your friend. It's nature's way of grabbing your attention and whispering, "Hey, maybe you can find a better way." It makes you aware of genuine threats while challenging you to find a smarter path.

> **You're venturing to a thrilling destination, and you need to be prudent. You need to be aware of the risks at every turn, carefully deciding which ones are worth taking and proceeding wisely.**

The key is to use fear as a tool to make informed decisions without letting it paralyze you. Think of it as a key input of growth. Too little, and you might miss critical warning signs. Too much, and you'll never progress. The right amount is where magic happens.

Your job as a leader isn't to eliminate fear but to calculate the risks and proceed with educated, efficient decisions. By doing this, you transform fear from a roadblock to a trusted ally in your decision-making process.

What's the Worst That Can Happen?

Before we close this topic, I want to tell you about Tina Lum, the CEO of Vancouver-based Push Operations, a company that creates workforce management software for the restaurant industry. Tina says, "People tend to talk themselves out of opportunity. Our brains are designed to be attracted to negativity."

That's why she and her leadership team always sincerely ask, "What's the worst that can happen?" This simple question helps them distinguish between real threats and reflexive negativity. By keeping fear in check, they increased monthly recurring revenue fivefold in three years.

In a Nutshell

Fear is not your enemy—it's a valuable tool that helps you recognize genuine threats and make smarter decisions. But if you let it dominate decision-making, it will paralyze your business.

- The key to ongoing growth is finding the right mix: enough fear to keep the business safe, but substantial courage to keep moving forward with calculated risks.
- Remember that waiting for perfect conditions or complete certainty is a recipe for stagnation.
- At some point, you need to push through fear, test your hypotheses in the real world, and apply your lessons so the company grows.

Questions

What real or perceived fear is slowing your company down today?

_____

_____

_____

_____

_____

_____

_____

_____

_____

_____

_____

How could you intelligently minimize it?

_____

_____

_____

_____

_____

_____

_____

_____

_____

_____

_____

CHAPTER 5

The 4 Forces of Growth

Defying gravity isn't denying limits—it's
mastering what lifts you beyond them.

—Kevin Lawrence

Hang on to your hat because now we're going to do a little
physics. OK, not really . . . but sort of.

As we've established, your single biggest risk as the CEO of
a growing company is spatial disorientation: losing your focus
on Real Growth to problems or fear, and making the wrong
decisions as a result.

Here's the obvious question: How do you prevent spatial
disorientation?

At first glance it might seem as easy as not focusing on

problems and not being fearful anymore. But you already know that's not a practical answer. If you don't do enough problem-solving and risk-averting, you end up with an unstable, high-risk company that's not built for growth. You wind up with drama and lawsuits, and no CEO wants that.

> **Your single biggest risk as the CEO of a growing company is spatial disorientation: losing your focus on Real Growth to problems or fear, and making the wrong decisions as a result.**

Instead, you need to start with a deeper understanding of the forces that either generate your growth or destroy it.

Let's turn to aviation again as our metaphor, because it turns out that flying a plane and running a growing company have a great deal in common.

The 4 Forces of Flight

To keep a plane airborne, pilots need to harness the four forces of flight: lift, thrust, weight, and drag.

In extremely basic layperson terms (forgive me, physicists and aviators), to create altitude:

- **Lift** is generated by the wings of the plane. It allows the plane to ascend, counteracting the force of **weight**, which pulls the plane downward.

- The **thrust** of the engines pushes the plane forward. This counteracts **drag**, the resistance of air that slows the plane down.

Basically, the plane takes flight when thrust and lift overcome weight and drag.

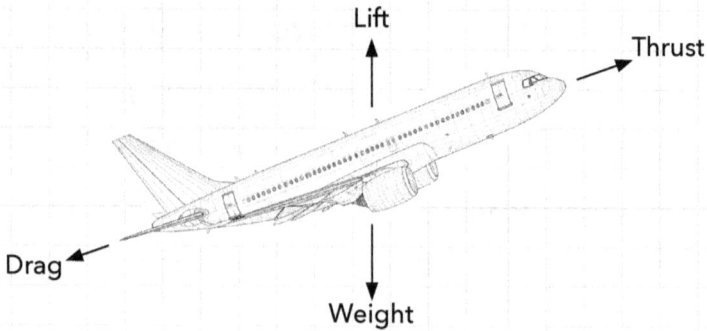

The 4 Forces of Growth

Just as planes don't magically stay airborne, companies don't just magically keep growing. Like a pilot, you're defying gravity.

In my role as a Growth Scientist, I've consistently observed that when CEOs invest significant amounts of the company's time, energy, and resources to sell more X's, their companies tend to stay aloft and continue growing. However, when too much time, energy, and resources shift to problem-solving or risk avoidance, growth slows or stops.

Given this, leaders need a fast, easy way to assess where time, energy, and resources are going so they can keep calibrating to Real Growth. That's why I created a model I call the 4 Forces of Growth.

To defy gravity as a CEO, you need to master these four forces:

1. **Opportunity:** Like the force of lift in aviation, *opportunity* elevates the company toward your long-term vision.
2. **Problems:** Like the force of weight, *problems* weigh the company down, opposing the force of opportunity.
3. **Courage:** Like the force of thrust, *courage* pushes the company forward.
4. **Fear:** Like the force of drag, *fear* slows the company down, opposing the force of courage.

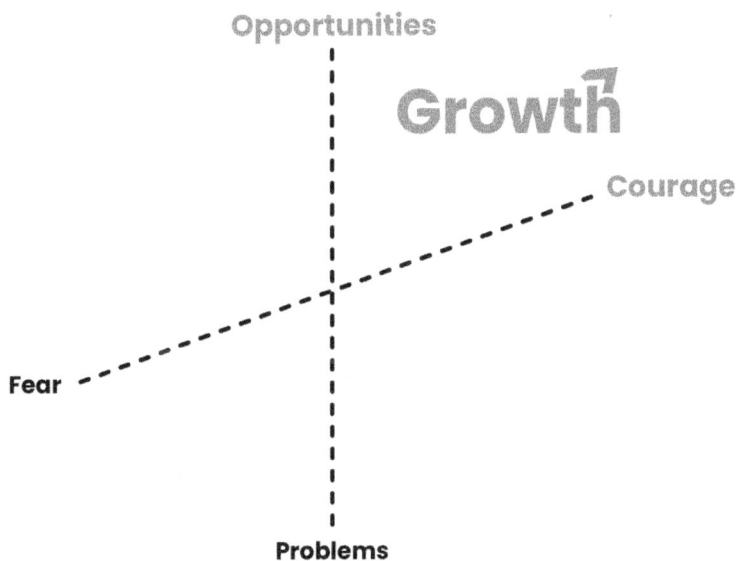

Now, pay close attention—this is crucial information. As a CEO, you've got two levers that control the growth of your business: opportunities versus problems and courage versus fear.

Growth Lever #1: Opportunity vs. Problems

Your first lever controls how much the company focuses on opportunities versus problems.

When you push this lever too much in the direction of opportunity, the business becomes unstable because too many problems go unaddressed.

When you adjust this lever too much toward problems, the business doesn't grow much or at all. You're so focused on problems, you're not pursuing enough opportunities.

The key here is to constantly calibrate this lever so you have enough focus on opportunity to keep growing yet enough problem-solving to keep the business stable and thriving. And of course, this is tricky because there are never enough resources to address everything. Tough judgment calls must be made.

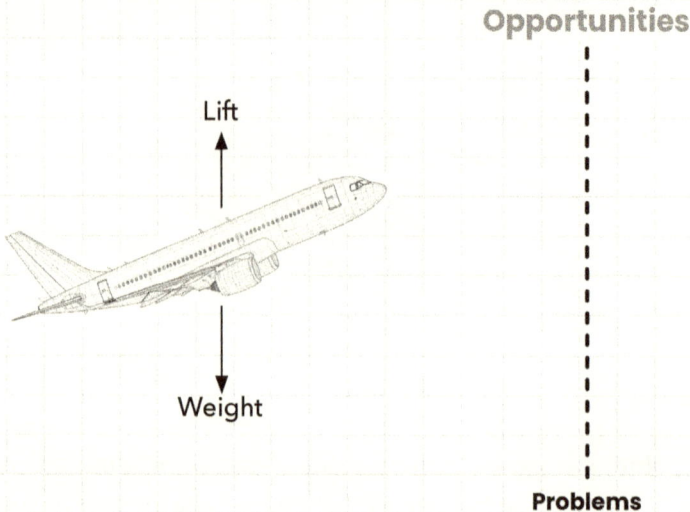

Growth Lever #2: Courage vs. Fear

Your second lever controls how much courage the company has versus fear.

When you adjust this lever too much in the direction of courage, you're not properly assessing and managing risks that could take the business down.

When you have too much fear, it becomes hard to move forward with anything, and the whole company slows down, limiting or stopping growth.

Your job is to constantly calibrate this lever so the company is courageously pursuing enough growth opportunities, while also having enough fear that you are averting real risks and making sound decisions.

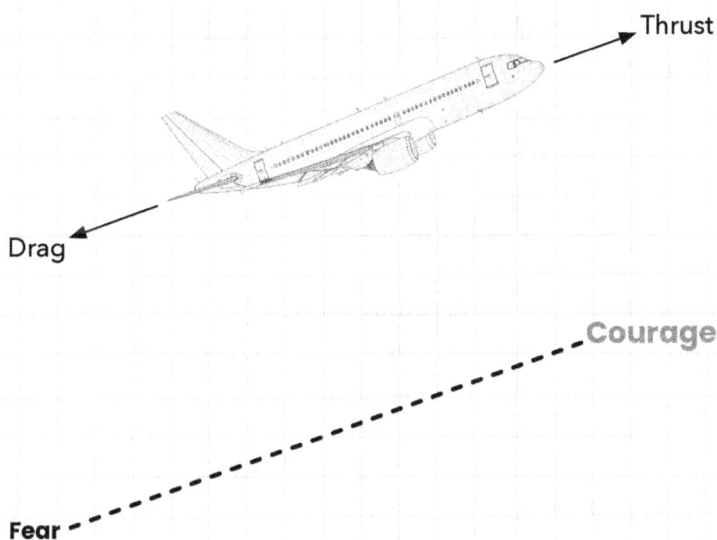

Navigating to Growth

Your levers control the direction and speed of your plane toward growth. Long-term growth only happens when you're constantly aware of these levers and adjusting to stay on course.

> **Just as planes don't magically stay airborne, companies don't just magically keep growing.**

You must adjust to what's happening in the market and within the company, making sure you're moving forward and upward prudently. Not going too fast or too slow. Being courageous with appropriate doses of fear to keep the company safe and sound.

If you're not carefully managing these levers, no matter how fantastic and hardworking your team is, the company may stall or end up in a nosedive.

To recap, as a CEO, you need to:

1. **Focus on opportunities to sell more X's** to drive Real Growth, but don't ignore the problems that could derail your business.
2. **Make courageous decisions**, but maintain enough fear to ensure those choices are informed and smart.

In a Nutshell

As a CEO, your biggest enemy isn't the competition or the economy. It's spatial disorientation—losing your bearings in the airspace of growth. When you're disoriented, problems and fear can hijack your focus, leading to bad decisions that send you off course and cause your team to underperform.

- The 4 Forces of Growth model is your compass. It helps you understand what you're up against: the constant push and pull of opportunity versus problems and courage versus fear.
- The answer isn't to ignore problems or banish fear. It's to maintain a clear-eyed view of all four forces so you can manage them.
- With the 4 Forces of Growth model, you can spot when you're veering off track and make the necessary adjustments to stay oriented toward growth.

Questions

What might you need to change to sustain growth long term?

_____

_____

_____

_____

_____

_____

Which specific opportunities could you focus more or less on?

_____

_____

_____

_____

_____

_____

Where could you lead with more or less courage?

_____

_____

_____

_____

_____

_____

CHAPTER 6

Mastering Growth

Instead of telling people what to
do, give them the knowledge and
tools to decide for themselves.

—Meg Whitman

When pilots fly, they don't constantly think about the four forces of flight. Instead, they focus on their flight instruments so they know when to recalibrate to stay on course. These instruments provide the information needed to make sure the plane is safe and on track.

Let's delve into how you can use the 4 Forces of Growth model as your flight instruments so you don't need to think abstractly about your growth levers, opportunities versus problems, and courage versus fear.

Using the 4 Forces of Growth

The 4 Forces of Growth model is the simplest, fastest way I know to get a strategic snapshot of a company's growth trajectory.

You can use it to visualize your resource allocation, allowing you to see at a glance where your resources are going. Based on this, you can quickly assess whether your efforts align with your growth objectives and make adjustments as needed.

Here's how it works. All the hard work you and your team do, and every investment you make, can be categorized into one of the four quadrants in the 4 Forces of Growth model:

Opportunities

Growth

Analysis

Courage

Fear

Agony *Improvement*

Problems

1. **The Growth Quadrant** includes all your resources devoted to selling more X's.
2. **The Improvement Quadrant** includes your resources devoted to increasing profit per X and improving operational efficiency.
3. **The Analysis Quadrant** includes resources devoted to evaluating opportunities, problems, and risks to inform decision-making.
4. **The Agony Quadrant** includes resources devoted to compliance, risk mitigation, and addressing actual or potential problems.

> **All the hard work you and your team do, and every investment you make, can be categorized into one of the four quadrants in the 4 Forces of Growth model.**

The 4 Forces Assessment

Are You Oriented Toward Growth?

This simple assessment helps you get a quick snapshot of your company's current orientation to growth. It's a fast way to understand your growth prospects.

When you assess your focus (where your time is going) and your team's focus (your strategic objectives), remember that I'm not asking where you *think* your resources are going. I'm asking you to determine where they are *actually* going.

The goal is to uncover the truth about your current focus and whether it aligns with your growth aspirations. There's often a gap between intention and reality.

To assess your orientation:

1. **Look at your Real Growth data:** How many X's did you sell annually for the past five years? What was your annual profit or gross profit per X for the past five years?
2. **Look at your calendar:** What percent of your time is spent in each quadrant?
3. **Look at your strategic plan:** What percent of your objectives are in each quadrant?
4. **Look at your communication:** What percent of your conversations with your direct team and the rest of the company is related to each quadrant?

Your Numbers: X and Profit per X

Your Real Growth data	Annual X's sold	Annual profit or profit per X
Current year		
2 years ago		
3 years ago		
4 years ago		
5 years ago		

Your Time

Percent of your average month spent in each quadrant	Last few months	Ideal based on growth ambitions
Growth (more X's)		
Improvement (profit per X)		
Analysis		
Agony		

Your Strategic Plan

Percent of strategic plan objectives in each quadrant	This year	Ideal based on growth ambitions
Growth (more X's)		
Improvement (profit per X)		
Analysis		
Agony		

Your Communication

Percent of your internal communication in each quadrant	Last few months	Ideal based on growth ambitions
Growth (more X's)		
Improvement (profit per X)		
Analysis		
Agony		

Other things to consider:

- **Executive team:** Percent of meeting time/agendas spent on growth (selling more X's) versus other quadrants
- **New hires and promotions:** Percent allocated to growth
- **Internal communications:** Percent about growth
- **Internal recognition:** Percent for growth
- **Capital investments:** Percent to drive growth
- **Reporting:** Percent weekly and monthly reporting that shows growth
- **Strategic discussions:** Percent about growth

Your Unique Mix

This brings me to the crux of the matter. If you want your company to grow, you must have significant resources allocated to the Growth Quadrant. It really is as simple as that.

However, it's crucial to understand that the goal isn't to funnel all your resources into the Growth Quadrant. Definitely not. This would destabilize and ultimately destroy the business. Instead, resources need to be consciously and strategically distributed across all four quadrants. This is why I say your business should be *oriented toward* the Growth Quadrant rather than *in* the Growth Quadrant.

> **Resources need to be consciously and strategically distributed across all four quadrants.**

It's also not the goal to equally distribute your resources across the four quadrants.

The key is to find your unique allocation mix, investing enough to achieve your growth goals while maintaining a healthy and stable business. When you've found your optimal mix, your company is positioned for long-term, sustainable Real Growth.

Your specific mix is determined by:

- How much and how fast you want to grow
- What drives your growth
- How well your company is operating today
- How ready your people and systems are to handle additional growth
- What challenges you're facing in the market

As CEO, you must constantly ask: Am I investing enough in growth? Because over time, most CEOs inadvertently shift more resources to improvement at the expense of growth.

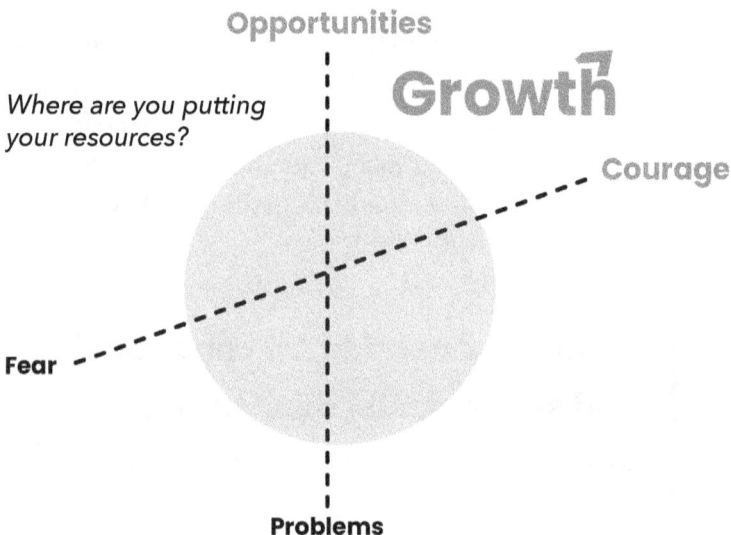

Opportunities

Growth

Where are you putting your resources?

Courage

Fear

Problems

The 4 Forces of Growth Assessment

To assess where your company's resources are
currently going, take the 4 Forces of Growth
assessment at 4forcesofgrowth.com.

Juan's Story

I'm going to put the 4 Forces of Growth model in context for
you. Let's start with *Juan.

A former-athlete-turned-CEO, Juan was frustrated by the
state of his business. After a decade in the sports retail industry, he and his execs had built a substantial enterprise and
were one of the top three competitors in their niche. But for
reasons that eluded them, they'd hit a plateau. They wanted
to get back on track to doubling the business in the next four
years.

I asked them to tell me their top three long-range priorities. They debated vigorously until I finally interjected.

"Let's break it down," I suggested. "What percent of the
company's resources are devoted to selling more X's? And
what percent goes to improving operations?"

They calculated they were devoting less than 10 percent
of their resources to selling more X's and about 70 percent to
improvements, with the rest divided between the Analysis and
Agony Quadrants. These were not the numbers they expected
or intended. They'd simply never thought about their business
through the lens of resource allocation before.

Juan noted he was personally spending less than 20 percent of his time on growth activities. Instead, he spent most

of his time managing store operations, fine-tuning inventory systems, and solving day-to-day staffing challenges. This was far from ideal in his role as chief visionary and starting quarterback.

Here's how Juan's company looked using the 4 Forces of Growth model—you can see he was placing most resources in the Improvement Quadrant:

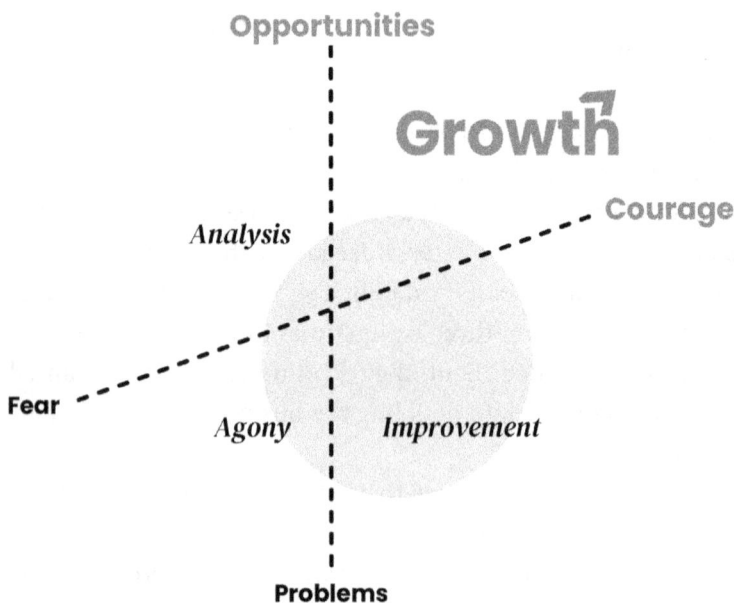

Like many great teams, Juan and his execs were making an assumption that spreading resources across key areas of the business would generate the growth and stability they desired. Instead, it was diluting their efforts. They were doing tons of amazing work, but too much fell into the category of improvement.

To be clear, there was nothing inherently wrong with his team's percentages toward growth and improvement. Those numbers may be ideal for some companies. But with a desire to double the company's size in a competitive marketplace, Juan's team simply wasn't investing enough in growth to get there.

> **Like many great teams, Juan and his execs were making an assumption that spreading resources across key areas of the business would generate the growth and stability they desired.**

The Shift

Juan's team pivoted immediately. They tripled their focus on growth activities, increasing from 10 percent to 30 percent of their total resources. This meant simplifying their strategic plan from twelve initiatives to three key projects. They postponed their store renovation program and put their inventory management system upgrade on hold—both nonessential projects that could wait.

Juan handed over store operations to his newly promoted COO. This eventually allowed Juan to spend about 50 percent of his time on growth—attending CEO summits in the sporting goods industry, exploring partnerships with major athletic brands, meeting with high-volume customers, and investigating expansion opportunities in neighbouring states. Rather than overseeing daily operations, he was finally doing what a CEO should: building the company's future.

Here's how his company looks now on the 4 Forces of Growth model. You'll notice considerably more resources devoted to the Growth Quadrant:

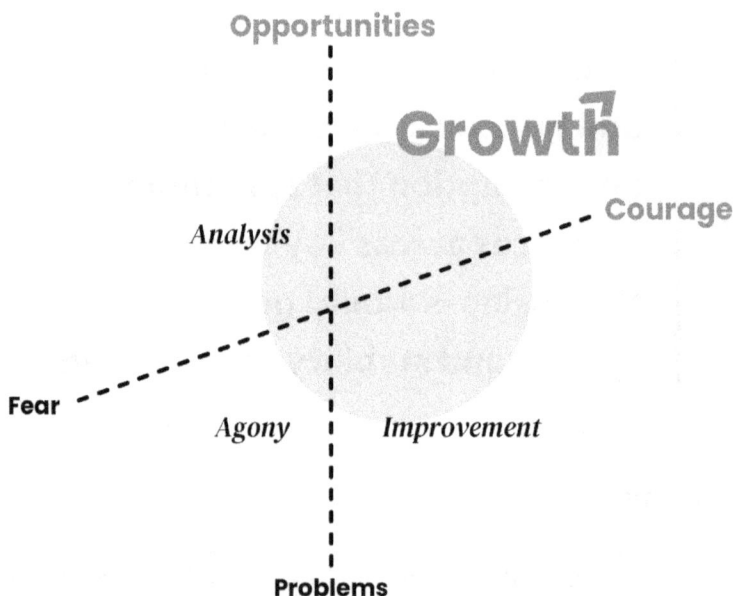

How to Use the 4 Forces of Growth Model

As a CEO, you must be constantly aware of how many resources are devoted to each quadrant. Using the 4 Forces of Growth model, a decline in growth is foreseeable and preventable. If too many resources go to places other than the Growth Quadrant, growth slows or stops.

This technique is a practical way to maintain a healthy mix of seizing opportunities, solving problems, analyzing decisions, and managing risks.

Viewing your business through this lens helps you improve your decision-making so you can stay aligned to Real

Growth. It helps you determine which initiatives to pursue and which to pass on. It helps you see how each choice affects your growth trajectory.

But it's important to know, this isn't a set-it-and-forget-it situation. You need to constantly recalibrate depending on what's happening in the business and the market, just like a pilot adjusts to changes in weather.

Your Secret Weapon Is Time

I cannot emphasize this enough: As CEO, your focus is one of your company's most precious resources. If you aim to grow your business substantially, the Growth Quadrant should be your primary responsibility. More than 50 percent of your time and energy should be devoted to growth.

When your company is set up for growth, your role is to rally your team around a big, exciting long-term vision and medium-term strategy.

This means you're an explorer of possibilities. You're out in the world learning, discovering, and identifying where the company will venture next. You spend time with customers and partners, absorbing market signals and emerging trends. You forge new strategic relationships that could reshape your company's future. You immerse yourself in conferences and learning events, not just as an attendee but as a seeker of opportunity.

> **I cannot emphasize this enough: As CEO, your focus is one of your company's most precious resources.**

You have space to think deeply and strategize. When major deals emerge, you're there to help close them. You thoughtfully direct the company's resources, ensuring growth initiatives receive the focus they deserve.

Your executive team also spends considerable time working in the Growth Quadrant, supporting the vision for the future.

As CEO, you know things are going well when:

- You're not spending much time in the Improvement Quadrant because you have an amazing executive team (and if the company is large enough, a president or COO) who handles day-to-day operations including almost all problem-solving.
- You're not spending much time in the Analysis Quadrant because your CFO is at the helm here, making sure you have the right data to make sound decisions.
- You're not spending much time in the Agony Quadrant because your legal counsel, compliance team, and/or human resources department is in charge of this, ensuring you're doing right by employees and regulators and abiding by the law.

With talented, capable executives in charge of the other quadrants, it's easy for you to stay focused on growth. Problems are dealt with before becoming dramatic. Steps are taken to ensure the company isn't incurring any unintended risks. Fear is in check.

In a Nutshell

The 4 Forces of Growth model gives you x-ray vision into your company's trajectory by showing you exactly where your resources are going. Like a pilot's flight instruments, it reveals if you're headed toward growth or drifting off course.

- The reality is simple but profound: Your company will achieve Real Growth only when you have significant resources devoted to the Growth Quadrant, including your time as CEO.
- Remember, the goal isn't to put all resources in the Growth Quadrant—that would destabilize the business.
- Instead, you need to be oriented toward growth while maintaining enough focus on improvement, analysis, and risk management to keep the business thriving.

Questions

If you recalibrated your resource allocation right now, where would you invest less to improve your growth orientation?

_____

_____

_____

_____

_____

_____

_____

Which specific things would you invest less in?

_____

_____

_____

_____

_____

_____

_____

Where would you reinvest those freed-up resources?

_____

_____

_____

_____

_____

_____

CHAPTER 7

Growth Detours

There is surely nothing quite so
useless as doing with great efficiency
what should not be done at all.

—Peter Drucker

When your company isn't oriented for growth, it's inevitably headed in another direction. But which one? And what are the implications?

In this chapter, we'll explore how to discern what's really going on in your organization by taking a look at the other quadrants of the 4 Forces of Growth model: the Improvement Quadrant, the Analysis Quadrant, and the Agony Quadrant.

Evaluating these quadrants tells you when your resource allocation isn't leading to long-term growth.

I have a disclaimer however. In times of turbulence, it may be necessary to lean heavily into one of these quadrants. For example, if your company is facing a massive product quality crisis or a customer service meltdown, it's important to temporarily channel extra resources into the Improvement Quadrant. If you're facing a compliance crisis or there's a major shift in the regulatory environment, you'd likely shift more resources to the Agony Quadrant.

But over the long term, a company can't divert resources from growth and expect to continue growing.

> **When your company isn't oriented for growth, it's inevitably headed in another direction.**

This chapter is about understanding when you've drifted from the path of growth without realizing it so you can recalibrate and make your way back.

The Improvement Quadrant

The most important thing for you to know about the Improvement Quadrant is that it can easily feel like you're in the Growth Quadrant. It's deceptive. It's the biggest danger zone for companies that want to grow.

You may accidentally overfocus on the Improvement Quadrant simply because it feels so darn good to hang out here. Teams with too many resources in the Improvement Quadrant often run an incredibly solid business, get rave reviews from customers, win awards for quality, and generate industry-leading profits. But over time they wonder why the company isn't growing like it used to. Here's what it can look like to have too many resources assigned to improvement:

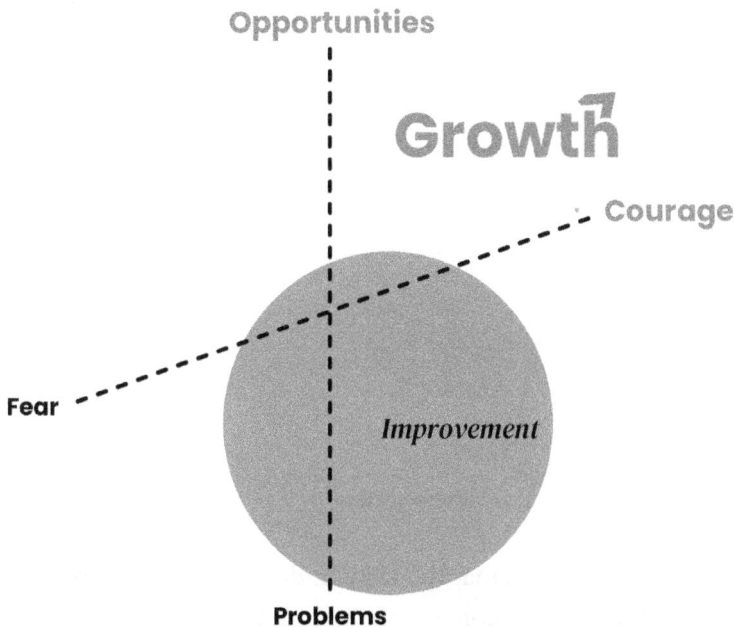

Opportunities

Growth

Courage

Fear

Improvement

Problems

Remember Tara from chapter 3? She's the CEO who fell in love with problem-solving and firefighting after her company was hit with a series of misfortunes, including the exit of two senior leaders. She was knee-deep in day-to-day operations, running tech projects and solving internal problems. She's an example of what it's like in the Improvement Quadrant.

The Analysis Quadrant

When a company has too many resources devoted to analyzing opportunities, risks, and other decisions, it moves at a snail's pace, and it is all but impossible to grow. It's oriented to the Analysis Quadrant. Here's what that may look like:

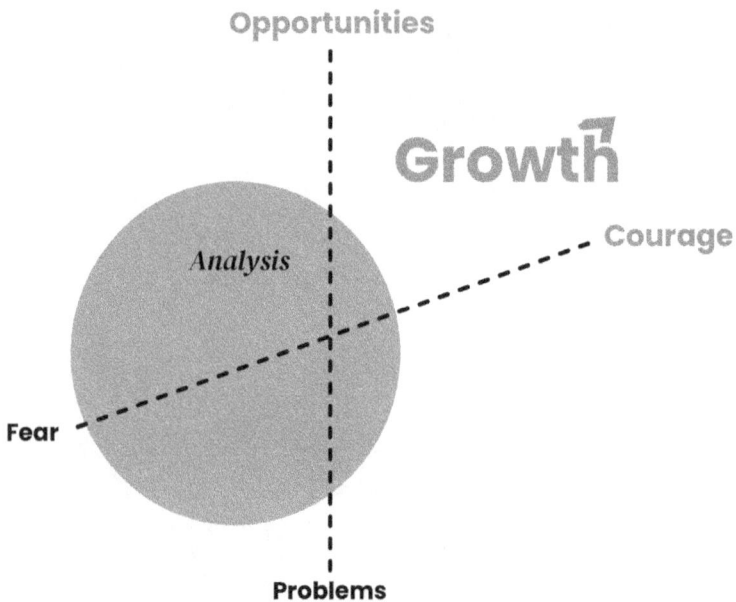

Remember Prishna, the fashion designer from chapter 4? After a failed expansion into the US market nearly bankrupted her business, she got stuck in analysis paralysis. She was constantly asking for more data and opinions and was unable to make swift decisions. Every opportunity that came her way was met with endless requests for market research, financial projections, and expert consultations. Even small decisions were arduous. Her once-nimble, successful fashion brand became stuck in perpetual planning mode. This is an example of what it's like in the Analysis Quadrant.

The Agony Quadrant

A company that's in the Agony Quadrant—well, the name says it all. This company is consumed with fear and worry, agonizing over everything. The executive team can't agree on a direction because everyone sees risk in every corner.

Here's what it may look like when you have too many resources in the Agony Quadrant:

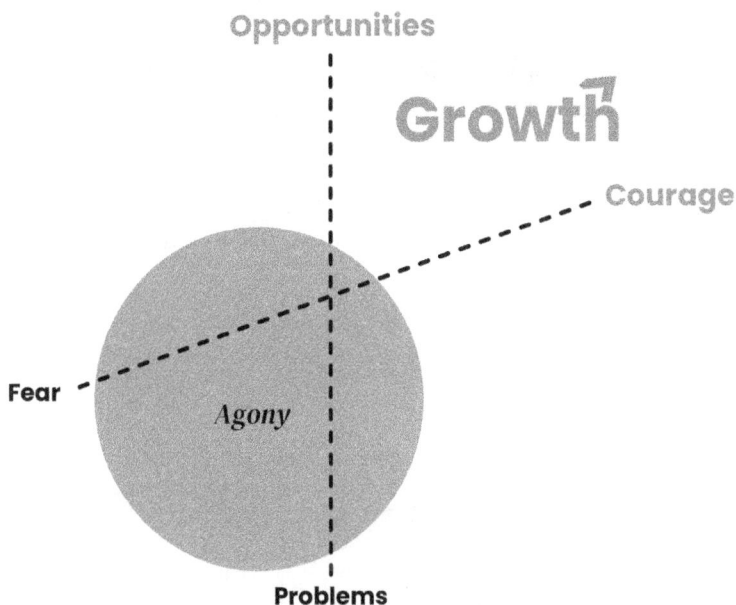

In chapter 4, we met Dan, the CEO of a structural engineering firm. He was burned out by a series of personal and professional trials, including lawsuits and betrayals. When presented with the chance to expand to a new niche, he could perceive only the risks. Every bright possibility was deflated by fret and exhaustion. His firm, which had been thriving, became bogged down by fear. This is an example of living in the Agony Quadrant.

Reckless Growth

Lastly, some companies focus almost solely on chasing opportunities. These teams are growth oriented and courageous to a fault.

They expand fast, but they ignore problems and throw caution to the wind. No risk is too big. These cliff-divers view anyone who dares to raise a concern as a pessimist and naysayer. A team like this is a party on wheels until the day fate comes calling and everything comes crashing down.

Here's what it looks like to devote too many resources to the Growth Quadrant and blast your company straight out of the sky:

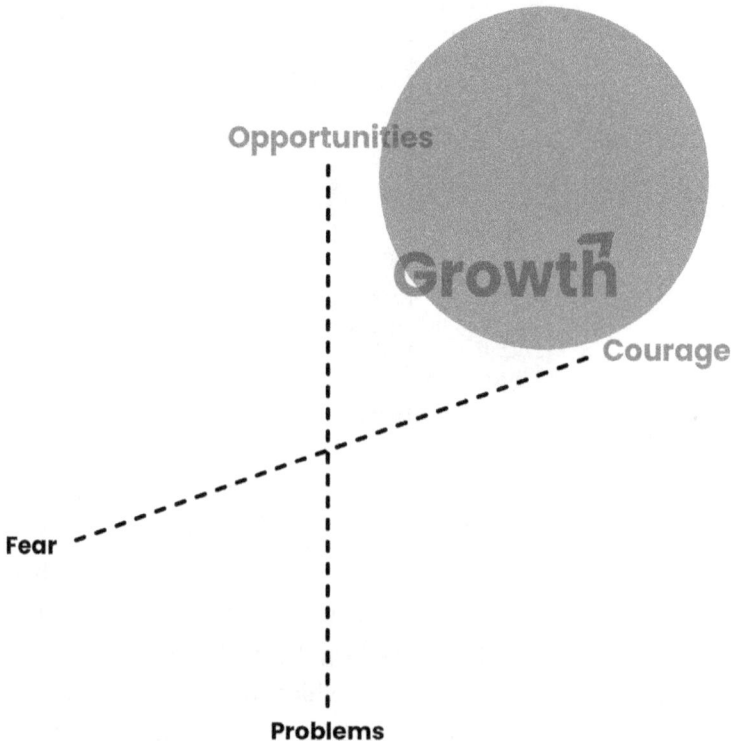

I'll give you the example of a CEO named *Michael. He started with two boutique fitness studios in San Francisco, known for high-intensity training programs and a fiercely loyal clientele.

Intoxicated by his success and flush with investor cash, he expanded to twenty-two locations across the West Coast in eighteen months.

But Michael didn't have the systems, processes, or leadership talent to support such rapid growth. His proprietary training programs became diluted. Customer experience varied wildly between locations. His pristine brand reputation crumbled as negative reviews piled up.

Within two years, he was forced into bankruptcy, leaving hundreds of employees jobless. His is a classic tale of reckless growth.

> **Aggressive growth pushes boundaries but maintains safeguards. Reckless growth is simply that—reckless.**

Aggressive Growth vs. Reckless Growth

My team and I work with many CEOs who constantly push the limits of growth, always striving to grow faster. It's an admirable trait, but it raises the question: How do you know when you're pushing too far too fast?

Three variables tell you if you're pushing beyond your company's capabilities:

1. **Leadership capacity:** Do you have highly effective senior leaders in your most important roles? Your leadership team is the engine that drives growth.
2. **Operational infrastructure:** Are your systems and processes robust enough to consistently deliver on what you've promised customers?
3. **Financial runway:** Do you have the cash flow to continue funding the aspirations of your growing organization? Growth requires investment, and without adequate financial resources, your expansion plans can quickly hit a wall.

Successful companies generally maintain additional capacity in all three areas. They always have a Plan B and often a Plan C. To me, this marks the crucial difference between aggressive growth and reckless growth. Aggressive growth pushes boundaries but maintains safeguards. Reckless growth is simply that—reckless.

In a Nutshell

When leaders lose a grip on Real Growth, they've drifted too far into one of three zones:

- The Improvement Quadrant (focused on making things better)
- The Analysis Quadrant (stuck in endless evaluation)
- The Agony Quadrant (paralyzed by fear and worry)

Equally dangerous is focusing solely on growth while ignoring operational stability. This is reckless growth, and it eventually leads to disaster.

Questions

Which quadrant does your organization naturally gravitate to?

_____
_____
_____
_____
_____
_____
_____

Which quadrant tends to get neglected by you?

_____
_____
_____
_____
_____
_____
_____

By your organization?

_____
_____
_____
_____
_____
_____
_____

PART 2

Staying in the Growth Quadrant

Resisting Fear and Problems

Be deliberate about every choice
you make. Time, energy, and
focus are finite resources.

—Sheryl Sandberg

Understanding the 4 Forces of Growth is only your first step. Knowing is wonderful, but it doesn't mean much if it doesn't translate into action.

Now that you grasp the 4 Forces of Growth and the pitfalls that can derail even the most promising companies, the next question is: What practical steps can you take to stay on your path of growth?

Keep reading because things are about to get real. In the following chapters, I share the exact approaches my team and I apply with clients day in and day out to help them grow continually. These are the frameworks and tools we always come back to because the results are undeniable. They've been proven across industries and geographies, time and again.

The following chapters will help you resist the gravitational pull of problems and fear so you maintain your trajectory to growth, no matter what. Here's the breakdown:

- **Chapter 8: The Battle of Two Bicycles** explains why even the most capable CEOs struggle to maintain their focus on growth, and how this pulls them away from the Growth Quadrant into the Improvement Quadrant.
- **Chapter 9: The Problem of Pond Hockey** shows how loyalty can become your greatest obstacle to growth and why upgrading your team requires courage most CEOs lack.
- **Chapter 10: The Impulse to Improvise** explores the hidden dangers of creativity and complexity that can divert your attention from what truly drives growth.
- **Chapter 11: The Neurosis of Numbers** helps you make better, faster decisions so you don't get stuck in the Analysis Quadrant.

Let's begin with "The Battle of Two Bicycles."

CHAPTER 8

The Battle of Two Bicycles

He who chases two rabbits
catches neither.

—Confucius

Picture this: You're a cyclist preparing for a major race. You've trained hard, you know the route, and you're feeling pumped. But when the big day comes, you're suddenly told the challenge isn't to ride just one bike but to ride two simultaneously.

Does this sound like sheer madness to you? Does it sound like a complete impossibility? Well, many CEOs try to ride two bikes at once every single day.

Let me tell you about *Alex, a CEO I met in Texas. His solar panel company made a huge mark in the renewable energy sector in large part due to Alex's engineering excellence and top-notch operational skills.

But his business had taken a recent turn. He told me, "Kevin, we're more profitable than ever, but we've hit a wall. Competitors keep beating us in deals we should win."

Glancing around the room, I saw solar panel prototypes strewn about, surrounded by testing equipment. Tools were scattered across Alex's desk. The whole place felt more like a shop floor than a corner office.

"When was the last time you spoke with a potential customer or attended an industry conference?" I asked, suspecting I already knew the answer.

Alex responded, "Look, I'm obviously knee-deep in product development. I don't have time for conferences or networking."

This duality is what I call the Battle of Two Bicycles, and it's one of the biggest reasons great companies stop growing. Alex was dealing with the quintessential CEO struggle of managing internal initiatives while guiding the company's future. You see, as a CEO, you actually have two giant jobs, not just one.

> **It's not about working harder. It's about recognizing that trying to ride both bicycles at once compromises your performance on each.**

The Two Giant Jobs

Giant Job #1
The Operational Bicycle–Running the Business

The Role of President or COO
Key accountability: Sustaining and ideally increasing profit per X

This role is about today's performance. It's overseeing and improving day-to-day operations. This role demands a boots-on-the ground, immediate-term mentality. It's living up to sales quotas, making payroll, improving products, and keeping customers happy. This role is primarily in the Improvement Quadrant, and many CEOs get dragged into spending 95 percent of their time here. In fact, many CEOs are stuck here, unable to free themselves from these responsibilities.

Giant Job #2
The Strategic Bicycle–Growing the Business

The Actual CEO Job
Key accountability: Selling more X's

This role is about future growth. It's planning for where the business will be five years from now. It's the Growth Quadrant part of the job, and it's often neglected. This role requires having your head in the sky, envisioning what's possible. It's meeting new people, bringing in new customers and partners, opening up new markets, courageously doing whatever it takes to sell more X's and drive Real Growth.

Most CEOs want to spend more time here but can't figure out how. Here's what I've learned: Consistent long-term growth happens only when CEOs spend more than half their time on the strategic bicycle.

But the answer isn't to work long hours and split your time evenly between operations and strategy. That won't solve it. It's not about working harder. It's about recognizing that trying to ride both bicycles at once compromises your performance on each.

Different Jobs, Different Mindsets

The two roles aren't just different jobs—they're entirely different mindsets. It's not about dividing time between operational tasks and strategic projects. It's about shifting your entire perspective.

Take Alex, our solar panel CEO. One minute, he's troubleshooting a new panel design. The next, he's raising capital and strategizing acquisitions. It's like switching between a microscope and a telescope—a complete change in worldview.

No wonder CEOs get disoriented juggling both. As companies evolve, straddling both jobs becomes increasingly challenging. When growth stops or slows, it's often because the strategic bicycle gets neglected, left behind while the CEO takes off on the operational bike. In companies where growth continues but profit fades, the CEO abandoned the operational bike.

Some CEOs physically remove themselves from the office to make this mental shift. They immerse themselves in the outside world, attending events and CEO summits to uncover new markets, identify partners, and close major deals. Sometimes they retreat to quiet cafés, take a long walk, or book a solo trip to shake off operational cobwebs and tap into strategic thinking.

In fact, many CEOs do their best strategic work outside the office. Away from the constant operational fires, they can finally give their strategic bicycle the attention it deserves.

For example, Alex started blocking off afternoons for strategy time. Sometimes he finds a scenic spot to think about the big picture in regard to partnerships and revenue models. Other times, he's out forging new connections to build his business. It's been a cornerstone of his company's renewed growth.

> **Consistent long-term growth happens only when CEOs spend more than half their time on the strategic bicycle.**

Growth Must Be 50 Percent of Your Focus

Here's the cold, hard truth: If you don't ride your strategic bicycle enough, your company can't be strategic because everyone else follows your lead.

To make matters worse, when you are not focused on growth, your competitors gain ground. Every day you spend solely on operations is a day your competitors might be capturing market share, innovating, and building new partnerships. This creates a compounding problem: The less you focus on growth, the harder growth becomes because your competitive advantages erode. You're not just standing still—you're falling behind.

As CEO, your primary focus must be riding that strategic bike to ensure your company continues to sell more X's over the long term. There's no way around this fundamental truth.

Here's how to tell whether you're spending enough time in the Growth Quadrant: Take a look at your calendar. Is more than 50 percent of your time focused on activities that will generate future growth?

I always advocate for CEOs to let go of the operational bicycle as soon as they can, even very early in the company's growth. This means building a stellar executive team or promoting or hiring a president or COO to handle operations.

If you're not quite there yet, you need to shift enough operational responsibilities to other members of your executive team to free up your time. All you need are three or four exceptional direct reports and a crystal-clear strategy.

In Alex's case, he empowered his existing COO to truly take control of the operational bicycle. Now he has time to explore new markets like energy storage solutions and smart grid technologies. He's built alliances with key players in the sector. In other words, he's spending most of his time in the Growth Quadrant.

A Sustainable Structure

Now, let me be abundantly clear: The solution to the two-bike problem isn't becoming a superhuman who rides two bicycles simultaneously.

As hard as you may try, and as smart and agile as you may be, you can masterfully ride only one bike at a time. Otherwise you'll end up crashing or, worse yet, going nowhere at all.

Instead, the key is to create a sustainable structure that allows you to be on your strategic bike. This requires having the courage to reorganize your company in a way that works for you.

For example, Dean Fraser is the CEO and cofounder of CDN Controls, an energy services company that grew from four people in 2011 to more than seven hundred employees across twelve locations today. Dean and his cofounder and COO, Nick Stewart, created a structure that works perfectly for them.

As Dean explains, "I live in the big-picture space, looking at the pipeline of opportunities and ensuring our vision is always at the forefront. Nick drives the operational side of our business and is exceptional at it. We are strengthened by one another, and we work to retain this careful equilibrium—it pushes our business forward."

This delineation of roles has been crucial to multiplying CDN's growth and market presence.

> **As hard as you may try, and as smart and agile as you may be, you can masterfully ride only one bike at a time.**

Even More Bikes

But wait, there's more. As if balancing these two bicycles weren't challenging enough, sometimes CEOs find themselves taking on a third or even a fourth bike when key executives underperform or leave the company.

This dilutes the CEO's focus on growth even more. We'll dive deeper into this phenomenon and its implications in the next chapter, "The Problem of Pond Hockey."

Riding the Strategic Bike

In my many years of working with leaders, here's what I've found to be the truest, most high-value responsibilities for any CEO:

1. **Articulating a compelling vision and strategy to win:** Along with your executive team, craft a clear, inspiring vision for your company's mid-term and long-term future. It should describe how you will win in the marketplace and reinforce the key tenets of your culture. Ensure this vision permeates every level of the organization. Your team should be excited about it and see how their work relates to it.

2. **Securing and allocating resources:** Anticipate and acquire the resources you'll need in the coming years to advance toward your vision and implement your strategy. This includes capital, talent, partners, and technology. Identifying these resources early positions your company for growth and resilience.

3. **Cultivating relationships:** Get out of the office and into the world at least two days a week. Connect with customers, explore partnerships, and investigate growth opportunities. These interactions aren't about immediate gains. They're about gathering market intelligence, building

strategic networks, helping close important deals, and shaping your company's future.

4. **Evolving as a leader:** Your growth as a leader directly influences your company's ability to grow. You'll need different knowledge and abilities two years from now. And then again two years after that. Engage in executive education, coaching, focused reading, and peer mentorship.

5. **Mitigating risks:** Make sure your company can survive pretty much anything, including a major disruption in your industry, regionally or globally—like rapid inflation, a pandemic, or a natural disaster. This means confronting the brutal facts, anticipating what could happen, and being ready to respond. It's having a strategic view of risk: understanding which risks are manageable and which could take the company out.

The 4 Forces CEO Assessment

To evaluate yourself as CEO, take the 4 Forces of Growth Assessment at 4forcesofgrowth.com.

In a Nutshell

Many CEOs face an impossible task: riding two bicycles at once—the operational bike of running the business and the strategic bike of growing it.

- While both roles are crucial, trying to ride both bikes simultaneously leads to disorientation and compromised performance in both areas. The company gets pulled away from the Growth Quadrant and into the Improvement Quadrant.
- Your company can't reach its growth potential if you're constantly dragged into operations instead of leading growth.
- The solution is to create a structure that allows you to spend more than 50 percent of your time on the strategic bicycle. Build an exceptional team to handle operations.

Questions

Which bicycle is your default? Why?

_____

_____

_____

_____

_____

_____

_____

_____

_____

What change would allow you to spend enough time on the strategic bike?

_____

_____

_____

_____

_____

_____

_____

_____

_____

_____

_____

_____

CHAPTER 9

The Problem of Pond Hockey

Hire brilliance to guide you,
not to be guided.

—Kevin Lawrence

In many parts of Canada, kids turn frozen ponds into impromptu hockey rinks. For some, it's a rite of passage. Kids from the local community converge, lugging hockey sticks and gloves, skates slung over their shoulders.

There's no formal team selection here. No tryouts, no cuts. The new kid who can barely skate? He's in. The quiet kid with lightning speed? She's playing too. Even little Ethan, who's probably too young to be out here but tagged along with his brother, gets to join. Skill levels vary wildly, but it doesn't matter. If you show up, you get to play. That's the rule of the pond.

Why am I telling you this? Pond hockey and business have a surprising thing in common: Many CEOs end up choosing their teams in much the same way.

People were at the right place at the right time and landed on your leadership team. Likely, they were a great fit for a while, learning and growing along with the company and helping you build a remarkable business.

> ## If you show up, you get to play. That's the rule of the pond.

But now your company is a totally different beast. It's bigger and more complicated. The challenges, opportunities, and risks are all heightened. This isn't pond hockey anymore. It's more like the NHL.

Shifting to an NHL Mentality

To keep a company growing, CEOs need to adopt what I call an NHL mentality, or a pro sports mentality. For those who may not know, the NHL is the National Hockey League in Canada and the United States.

To have an NHL mentality is to have the expectation that everyone on your leadership team is a true A-player.

My definition of an A-player is a leader who's exceptional in their specific role and a joy to work with. They earn an A for meeting or exceeding the expectations of their position, plus they earn an A for embodying your company's values and culture. No compromises. In business, as in sports, your team determines your success. The stronger your players, the more likely you are to win.

This is where many CEOs find themselves at a crossroads. It's a classic battle between fear and courage: the fear of upsetting loyal colleagues versus the courage to build an exceptional team.

Many CEOs unknowingly create a culture where loyalty supersedes performance, letting their fear of difficult conversations override their aspirations for growth. This single choice—whether to prioritize loyalty or performance—often determines if a company will keep growing.

Your instinct may be to stick with the team that brought you this far. It's comfortable, it's loyal, it's what you know. But to keep growing, you need to face the probable reality that some of the people who got you here might not get you where you're going next.

This is so challenging that some CEOs decide to give up their aspirations of growth entirely. Exhausted by underperforming executives, they decide to sell the company rather than go through the process of upgrading the team.

Take Amish Shah, the CEO of Indiana-based Kem Krest, for instance. After years of success, Amish had become frustrated with the complexity of running his automotive supply chain company.

I suggested we do a full assessment of his executive team, and it was obvious Amish was stuck in a grand scale version of pond hockey. The team hadn't elevated their skills to match the company's growth and complexity, although they were excellent human beings.

We had some tough conversations, and within eighteen months, Amish replaced every senior leader with fresh talent suited to the company's size, challenges, and aspirations.

This brave move, combined with a simplified strategy, led Kem Krest back to record growth and profitability. Amish was able to focus on the strategic aspects of his job, reigniting his love of the business.

In Ontario, the Kim siblings at Cloré Beauty Supply also understand the power of A-players. When Jina and Clemens took over the family business from their father, they realized they needed to upgrade their leadership.

My team worked with Cloré to implement rigorous new hiring practices. In just over two years, they increased the A-players in leadership roles from 27 percent to 78 percent. Jina and Clemens were able to step back from being Chief Problem Solvers and start spending time on strategy.

"Before, the A-player mentality wasn't there," Jina told me. "But if you'd asked us, Is everyone an A-player? We would have said, yeah." This is why it's critical to learn what an A-player truly looks like for all your key roles.

> **You need to face the probable reality that some of the people who got you here might not get you where you're going next.**

The 90 Percent Rule

If you implement just one idea from this book, let it be this: 90 percent of your key leaders must be A-players, just like a pro sports team. Adopting this one rule has the power to revolutionize your business.

Building an NHL-calibre team requires unwavering belief. You must believe you can assemble such a team and, even more importantly, that you deserve one.

But it's critical to be practical. Don't try to build a full company of A-players overnight. Start with your key leaders, the people who most impact the performance of your business. These are the individuals who report to you and the key individuals who report to them.

A-players and Everyone Else

Here's a simple performance rating system to help you get clear on where you are today:

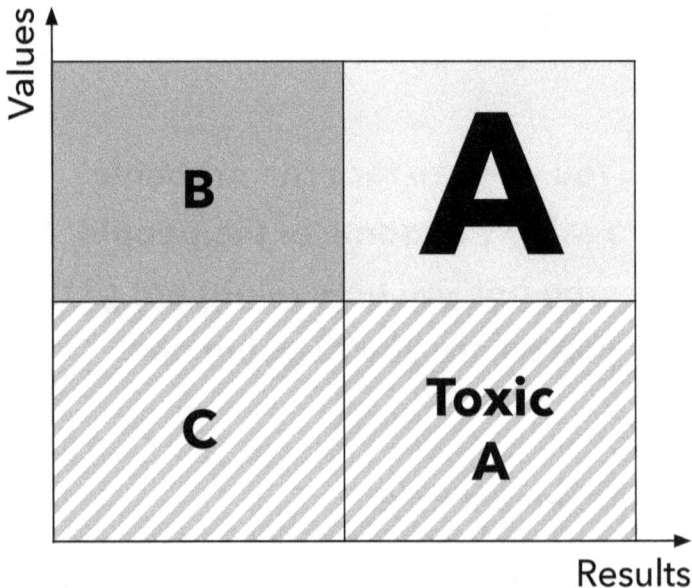

- **A-player:** Fits the culture and always delivers exceptional results with little or no management.

An absolute pleasure to work with. You wish you could clone them.

- **Toxic A-player:** Excellent performance, but regularly causes friction and drama because they don't fit the culture.
- **B-player:** A culture fit with spotty performance, whose leader backfills for them.
- **C-player:** Doesn't fit the culture or deliver results.

Remember this crucial point: the NHL mentality is not your HR team's job. It starts and ends with you, the CEO. You must champion this vision. Even the most skilled HR leaders will offer resistance because this approach makes their role at least twice as hard.

Organic Growth, Digital Pain

Now, let me tell you about *Mark, the founder of a chain of high-end organic grocery stores. Mark started the company with close colleagues from a previous job. They had one simple but beautiful store that blossomed into a network of fifty locations.

With online grocery shopping booming, Mark knew the company needed to adapt. So he cooked up a strategy to bring organic offerings to customers' doorsteps. But he found himself facing an unexpected opponent: resistance from within.

His COO couldn't fathom how their elegant in-store experience could translate to online shopping, and he feared mayhem with their inventory systems. His CFO was skeptical about the investment required for the online business. And his long-time marketing director was overwhelmed in his job as it was, never mind taking on a whole new initiative.

Mark spent time with each leader, diligently coaching them on what was required to support the initiative. He spent hours navigating resistance and internal conflicts. Executive meetings became part battleground, part therapy session.

By the time Mark called me, he was on the verge of giving up the digital venture completely, selling his majority stake in the chain, and taking an early retirement.

I worked with him over a period of a few months on a deep-dive assessment of his leadership team, and it became abundantly clear the business needed more than just a digital transformation. It needed a team transformation.

I want you to know, the leaders on Mark's team were all phenomenal people and genuinely skilled. The company had simply outgrown them. As a result, Mark was pitching in to help run almost every aspect of his business. He couldn't focus on his actual role as CEO because he was supporting every other leader.

After careful consideration, Mark made the painful but courageous decision to respectfully transition several long-time leaders to different roles and hire new ones. He told me it was the hardest decision of his career, but he knew the time had come. He needed new people to take the business forward.

Now Mark has a team with the know-how and background to handle the company's current scope and vision, allowing him to spend most of his time in the Growth Quadrant.

> **Remember this crucial point: the NHL mentality is not your HR team's job. It starts and ends with you, the CEO.**

The Backfill Trap

Like Mark, many CEOs think backfilling for underperformers is simply part of the job. They don't realize there's another way, so they juggle three or four jobs instead of focusing on their strategic responsibilities.

Not only does this hinder the company's growth, but it makes the CEO's role burdensome and unfulfilling.

Why does this happen? Some CEOs can't envision what true A-players look like for every position, especially in a growing business. Others shy away from setting high standards, fearing they'll appear unreasonable. And some dodge tough conversations, reluctant to raise the bar or let people go.

But you need to know, if you're aiming for sustained growth, backfilling for a weak leader on your team isn't an option. It's always a dead end.

Making the Tough Calls

When I start working with CEOs, I typically find less than a third of the key leadership roles are filled by true A-players. Together, we work to develop existing talent, make strategic new hires, and sometimes make tough changes. This journey requires both commitment and courage from the CEO.

It's not that these CEOs don't see the need for change. In fact, they almost always know exactly what needs to be done. The real hurdle is confirming the step that's needed and taking action on these difficult decisions.

Let's take a moment here to bust a myth: Hollywood loves to portray CEOs as cold-hearted tyrants, but that's far from reality in my experience. The best CEOs I know are deeply compassionate and fiercely loyal. That's what makes them exceptional leaders. And it's precisely why these decisions are so emotionally taxing.

But here's the hard truth: As your company grows, you must keep making these difficult choices. You must constantly evolve your team, ensuring the right people are in the right positions at every stage of growth. Building an A-player team isn't a one-time event. It's an ongoing commitment to excellence.

A-players Hire More A-players

When your executives and their direct reports are all A-players, they'll keep hiring more A-players. It's a virtuous cycle.

A-players want to work with other high performers to boost their own game. They love to surround themselves with stellar people, and this raises the calibre of your company.

But let's say you've got only 50 percent A-players in your top roles. What happens then? Your A-players get frustrated with the B-players. And those B-players are unlikely to hire A-players—they don't want others to outshine them, and this weakens your whole enterprise.

> **Hold out for A-players.**
> **Don't compromise.**

So let's talk about some essential ingredients for creating your own NHL team of 90 percent A-players.

1. Know Your Top Thirty Roles

Identify your key leaders—the top thirty roles (approximately) in your organization, looking at today and three years ahead.

These are the people who report to you and the core people who report to them. Next, define what an A-player looks like for each of these roles—crystal clear, no ambiguity.

Please note that if your company is larger than a thousand people, you may have more than thirty top roles. If it's smaller than a hundred people, you may have fewer.

2. Expect 90 Percent to Be A-players

For your top thirty roles, set the bar high: 90 percent should be absolute A-players. As CEO, you have the job of ensuring that these people thrive. They're the heartbeat of your company's future—be personally in sync with each one. Scrutinize and recognize their performance regularly.

This is where most organizations fail, denying key leaders the frequent feedback and development they deserve to become or remain A-players.

I suggest managing these individuals with the same care you'd give your blue-chip investments. Track and nurture their performance quarterly by creating ninety-day mini-development plans for your direct reports and asking your executives to do the same for their top roles. Each plan should identify two or three specific areas for growth or engagement, whether it's expanding capabilities or deepening involvement in core initiatives.

> **This is where most organizations fail, denying key leaders the frequent feedback and development they deserve to become or remain A-players.**

When performance gaps emerge, take fast action through mentoring, development, or difficult conversations. If necessary, make the hard decision to move or replace those who consistently fall short.

3. Your Existing Leaders Are Your Scouts

Every business faces the same challenge: finding great talent. For key roles, internal talent development often doesn't cut it. So you'll likely need to bring in some experienced outsiders.

But here's the common pitfall: Most CEOs turn to HR, who hire recruiters for these key roles. But your senior leaders have (or should have) the networks to find the best talent.

As a CEO, you'll greatly benefit from tasking your executives with constant talent scouting, ensuring you're never starting from zero when it's time to hire. Ideally, make this a mandate.

When you've exhausted the networks of your core team, it's the right time to seek help from recruiters.

> ## Every business faces the same challenge: finding great talent.

4. Have 90 Percent Confidence in Them or Pass

Too often when hiring or promoting for key roles, we compromise because of time pressure or a scarcity mindset. This is a fatal mistake. Here are two common scenarios to avoid:

- Hiring or promoting someone you think will be amazing, but missing red flags because the process is rushed or not diligent enough.

- Settling for a mediocre candidate due to time pressure, knowing they're not ideal for the role.

Your new mantra: Hold out for A-players. Don't compromise. Every key leader can impact your business by millions of dollars, so treat each one like a million-dollar investment.

There are always exceptional candidates available for any role. Always. But you may need to invest considerable patience and effort.

Resist the urge to make short-term, ill-advised decisions. A-players may take more time to find, but their long-term impact far outweighs the effort.

5. Use Fractionals and Experts

Even with a remarkable team, sometimes you need specialized expertise. Leveraging fractional executives and experts can be a game-changer. They can be used to:

- **Bridge gaps:** Need a new CFO, but hiring will take months? Bring in a temporary fractional CFO.
- **Scale expertise:** Sometimes you need high-level skills before you can justify a full-time hire. Get a consultant or fractional executive.
- **Make deep dives and big decisions:** Use consultants to analyze complex decisions or manage projects your team is too busy to tackle. This lets you move forward with new initiatives without overextending your core team.

In a Nutshell

Staying oriented toward the Growth Quadrant requires moving beyond pond hockey—where loyalty and familiarity drive team selection—to an NHL mentality, where exceptional performance is the standard.

- Surround yourself with A-players—exceptional people you love working with. This is key to sustaining Real Growth.
- You need A-players in 90 percent of your top thirty roles so you and your executives can focus on growing the company rather than backfilling for underperformers.
- This unlocks your full potential as a CEO and allows you to spend more than 50 percent of your time on your strategic bicycle.

Questions

What percent of your top thirty roles are A-players?

_____

_____

_____

_____

_____

What key leader do you need to add to your organization?

_____

_____

_____

_____

_____

Remove from your organization?

_____

_____

_____

_____

_____

Change roles?

_____

_____

_____

_____

CHAPTER 10

The Impulse to Improvise

Do less, then obsess.

—Morten Hansen

Picture yourself at an intimate jazz club. The lights dim, casting a warm glow through the room as a small ensemble takes the stage.

As they launch into their first number, you're instantly hooked by the melody. But it's the improvisation that truly captures you. Each musician, in turn, appears in the spotlight, weaving a solo that seems to emerge from the heavens. This is jazz at its finest—a delicate balance of structure and spontaneity, where each performance is a unique, unrepeatable moment.

Now, shift your gaze to a grand concert hall. A sea of musicians sit poised, instruments at the ready. The conductor ascends to the podium, raises her baton, and with a flick of her wrist unleashes a torrent of sound. Hundreds of musicians move as one, their individual parts blending magnificently.

This is a different kind of magic. It demands flawless coordination. Every note is predetermined, every phrase meticulously planned. The musicians follow sheet music to a tee, their eyes darting between the notes and the conductor's guiding hands.

For many companies, strategy is highly improvisational for years. There's often a blend of formal strategic planning and informal strategic detours. This can work when your business is relatively small—you can hash out a new market strategy over morning coffee and have it in motion by late afternoon.

But then the business grows. Soon you have too many people bringing too many ideas, innovations, and stand-alone initiatives. Instead of magnificent music, you now have a noisy, disagreeable mess.

Some leaders believe strategy necessarily becomes more complicated as a business grows. But in my experience, as you grow, your strategy needs to get simpler and clearer, protected from a constant flood of new ideas. This allows you to make the biggest market impact you can with your resources. It allows you to execute with laser precision.

Maestro of Growth

When your company reaches a certain size, typically about a hundred people, the CEO needs to become an orchestra conductor, aligning everyone to a single vision and strategy. Like a conductor, you've got to choose the set list, distribute the sheet music, and—most importantly—protect your vision from constant modifications and additions that muddy the music.

As a conductor, you wouldn't let musicians spontaneously change the symphony mid-performance or add their own interpretations whenever inspiration strikes. Instead, you would channel their creativity and talent toward the chosen work.

The same principle applies to your strategy. Your role isn't to shut down creativity or innovation—it's to direct everyone's energy and resources toward executing your chosen moves with precision. This means learning to say no to good ideas that don't align with your strategic focus. Even brilliant suggestions from senior leaders need to be carefully filtered.

My client *Simi learned this the hard way. Her cloud-based B2B tech company grew from a basement operation to a three-hundred-person powerhouse in five years, landing some big brand clients. She was living the entrepreneur's dream.

To keep up with the growth, she kept adding brilliant executives from tech giants like Oracle and Salesforce. At first, this seemed ideal; she wanted fresh perspectives and innovative ideas from experienced leaders. But soon it became clear that the executives weren't just bringing expertise—they were bringing entirely different visions for the company's future.

At first, Simi worked tirelessly to incorporate everyone's ideas, testing every strategic planning tool she could find. When that proved overwhelming, she gave her executives autonomy to pursue their own directions. This left her with disconnected strategies that were impossible to track or measure. Her once-nimble company started to feel like a bureaucratic giant.

Determined to fix the situation, Simi did what many CEOs do: she called in the cavalry. She hired a whiz-bang strategy consultant whose TED Talk was viral in business circles. The consultant swept in with a team of analysts, promising to craft the ultimate growth strategy.

Three months and seven figures later, Simi received a gleaming seventy-five-page document, complete with fancy infographics and enough jargon to fill a dictionary. When the consultant presented it to her team, everyone was entranced.

But two quarters later, there was still no headway. Her team was still trying to get the new strategy off the ground. Finally at her wit's end, Simi placed a call to me.

I took one look at the giant document and understood the problem. "No wonder your team's stuck," I said. "This isn't a strategy; it's a PhD thesis. It's brilliant, but you need a decoder ring to get past the executive summary."

> **As you grow, your strategy needs to get simpler and clearer, protected from a constant flood of new ideas.**

It took several weeks for me and my team to dig into Simi's business. We worked side by side with her and her executives to identify the three most consequential moves they could focus on for the next three years. This included establishing sales partnerships with four major tech vendors, rebuilding their core platform using next-generation technology, and creating an ongoing development program for current and emerging executives.

Then, we helped to create a simple system to protect these priorities from the never-ending flow of new ideas that had previously derailed their progress.

With that clear direction and protective framework in place, we crafted a simple strategy and detailed execution plan. The shift wasn't instant—it took the company about a year to get into the groove of working as a cohesive team rather than disconnected silos, but since then they've been outperforming their growth projections annually.

> **Your role isn't to shut down creativity or innovation—it's to direct everyone's energy and resources toward executing your chosen moves with precision.**

Yes, This Applies to You

In case this is on your mind, I often meet leaders who tell me their business is far too complex for a simple strategy. After thirty years in this business, I can tell you, this never holds true.

Every company can have a simple strategy if they approach it in a simple way. Having said this, simplicity is not easy. It's much harder to create a simple strategy than a complicated one because it requires clearer thinking, tougher decisions, and the discipline to protect it from new ideas.

As Mark Twain reportedly said, "I didn't have time to write a short letter, so I wrote a long one instead."

> **Every company can have a simple strategy if they approach it in a simple way.**

A Simple Strategy with Three Big Moves

In my experience, long-term growth is 20 percent strategy, 80 percent execution—but that 20 percent is absolutely mission critical.

When working with clients, my team and I craft a simple strategy using tools that fit their specific circumstances, industry, and corporate culture. After all these years, we have our preferred tools that drive results.

While it's impossible to generalize an exact route to your simple strategy, there are three core elements that are consistent and should be included in your plan: Vision, How We Win, and Three Big Moves.

Vision

Vision includes your values, purpose, and your Big Hairy Audacious Goal (BHAG). The concept of BHAG was introduced by Jim Collins in his book *Built to Last*, which was co-authored with Jerry Porras. It's a giant, long-term aspirational goal.

Most leaders know the importance of inspiring people with a big vision. But in reality, few companies have a vision that is compelling enough, authentic enough, and significant enough to drive Real Growth.

Too often, a vision becomes background noise, corporate fluff that hangs on a wall but doesn't influence daily decisions. When this happens, you miss a tremendous opportunity to align your teams and fuel your growth engine. A truly effective vision doesn't just describe what you do—it captures why it matters and how it creates value in the world.

In most cases, your vision isn't invention—it's archaeology. You need to excavate your core principles, dust them off, and, if needed, modernize them. Make them visible and known across the company so people are aligning all plans and actions to them.

How We Win

How We Win are the strategic principles that ensure your enduring competitive advantage.

Almost every growing business begins with a clear competitive advantage that leads to early success. But over time, this unique edge can get diluted—or even forgotten.

My team and I guide organizations to rediscover and sharpen their competitive edge using proven frameworks. We frequently draw on Jim Collins's hedgehog and flywheel concepts from *Good to Great* and *Great by Choice*, helping companies identify what they can be the best in the world at and what triggers their momentum. We also leverage tools from *Scaling Up* and *Blue Ocean Strategy* to clarify how to create distinctive value in the customers' eyes.

Three Big Moves

Three Big Moves, aligning to your Vision and How We Win, are the three projects, investments, or commitments that will double the company's size and strength in about three years. Something special happens when everyone in your organization aligns to your Three Big Moves. It creates harmony of effort, optimizing resources and results.

Let me tell you about a brilliantly simple Big Move. A Canadian company called Saje turned "Try before you buy" into an art form and goldmine. Jean-Pierre and Kate LeBlanc, the husband-and-wife founders (later joined by their daughter Kiara), built a solid retail brand selling a vast range of magnificent essential oils, natural remedies, and the like.

They knew whenever people experienced their formulations, magic happened. So they implemented a Big Move they called G-POP—Get Product on People. Sounds simple, right? It was. The move was to get the whole team laser focused on getting Saje products on people wherever they may be, especially their signature product, Peppermint Halo.

Walk into a Saje store? You'd get G-POPed—someone would roll a best-selling remedy on the back of your neck. Running a marathon? Maybe you'd get G-POPed at the finish line with a recovery blend for your tired muscles. People were G-POPed at yoga classes, sports events, trade shows—you name it.

When I first met Jean-Pierre, over twenty years ago, he was G-POPing a room of exhausted executives at a CEO summit, much to my amazement.

Saje's growth exploded across the country, growing from two stores in Vancouver to more than seventy locations across North America. This is a tremendous example of knowing what triggers Real Growth in your business and focusing on it relentlessly.

Something special happens when everyone in your organization aligns to your Three Big Moves. It creates harmony of effort, optimizing resources and results.

Ashiana's Big Moves

When Vishal, Ankur, and Varun Gupta took over Ashiana, their father's housing development company, they inherited more than just a business—they inherited his instinct for finding uncontested markets. Their father, Om, loved to go after niches with scarce competition, even if it meant venturing into unfamiliar terrain.

This mindset led Ashiana to make a Big Move in 2002. Although they'd always focused on housing for middle-income families in India, they decided to venture into a new category: senior housing. At the time, the move clashed with the prevailing belief that Indian families preferred to care for elderly parents at home. People questioned why Ashiana would focus on a market that supposedly didn't exist.

But Om and his sons saw what others missed: Demographic data showed that about 8 percent of Indian seniors were already living independently, and the number was growing as families became more affluent and geographically dispersed.

Like many Big Moves, Ashiana's leap into senior housing wasn't easy. The first project, in Bhiwadi, sold well but faced occupancy challenges. A second project, in Jaipur, struggled with sales. A third project, near Mumbai, ran into regulatory issues.

Instead of retreating, the Guptas dug deeper. They studied demographics more carefully and discovered that Chennai, in South India, had the perfect combination of factors for senior living to thrive. This insight led to a breakthrough project with rapid sales, proving the merit of their strategy. Meanwhile, the earlier projects gained traction as the market caught up to their vision.

The success of senior housing emboldened the Guptas to make another Big Move. Noticing India's increasingly affluent middle class spending heavily on children's education and development, they created another new category: kid-centric housing. These aren't just apartments with playgrounds—they are communities designed to help children thrive, with dedicated learning centres, spaces for art and music, and badminton courts that train state-level athletes.

Combined, Ashiana's two Big Moves transformed the business. Return on capital grew 35 to 40 percent year-on-year for seven years. And interestingly, when the general real estate market faced downturns, their specialized communities proved resilient. In one key market where housing sales dropped 90 percent, Ashiana's senior living projects not only continued to sell, but prices increased.

Today, senior living represents about 20 percent of Ashiana's sales volume and generates 20 to 30 percent of profits. Kid-centric housing has been a major hit, with one project alone accounting for 50 percent of profits. In total, the company now builds and sells about 1,800 to 2,000 new homes every year.

Choosing Your Three Big Moves

> The essence of strategy is choosing what not to do.
>
> *—Michael Porter*

Identifying your Three Big Moves might seem straightforward, but these are the toughest and most crucial decisions you'll make as a team. They form your blueprint for achieving desired growth in about three years. They are always tangible and measurable.

Often, Big Moves simply scale what already works for you—doubling down on your proven growth drivers. Sometimes they venture into new territory, like Ashiana's housing niches.

Specific examples include:

1. Growth
    - Growing from one hundred to five hundred salespeople
    - Adding fifty new Fortune 500 customers
    - Opening forty new locations
    - Expanding geographically
    - Moving into adjacent market segments
    - Launching a product that contributes 20 percent of revenue

2. Improvement
    - Doubling the leadership team's capabilities through development, hiring, and promotion
    - Reducing service costs by half
    - Building a new production facility to triple capacity
    - Improving specific customer experience metrics
    - Rebuilding core technology infrastructure
    - Making acquisitions to enhance capabilities
    - Transforming the customer service model

What unites these examples is scope and impact. These aren't quick fixes—they typically take years to implement and add millions to your bottom line.

To ensure your Big Moves stay on track, validate them annually as market conditions change. The key is to refine and adjust without overcomplicating—focus on making your moves better, not more numerous.

A Wildly Oversimplified Framework

At the risk of greatly oversimplifying, I'm going to share a high-level framework for thinking about your Three Big Moves. This is a starting point for your process.

After thousands of strategic planning sessions and knowing the long-term results, I've observed that effective Big Moves generally fall into these three categories:

1. **Drives more X's:** Growth moves that increase your X's and ultimately your sales volume
2. **Drives profit per X:** Improvements to how your business operates, enhancing quality, efficiency, and ultimately profits
3. **Strengthens your team:** Moves that build the capability and performance of your team

To be abundantly clear, I'm not suggesting you simply pick a move in each category and call it a day. Definitely not.

My team spends days researching Big Moves for our clients. We hold multiple sessions with the CEO and executive team to nail the right three choices. Determining the right moves for your company isn't a thirty-minute exercise. It's a serious undertaking.

Here are the criteria for success so you can get your Big Moves right:

- Each should improve annual profit by 10 to 20 percent through increased X's or profit per X.

- Each should be clear and measurable.
- Each should be simple enough for any capable businessperson to understand.
- First, focus on scaling what already works. Then, test new things.

For a more comprehensive methodology for choosing your Big Moves, visit 4forcesofgrowth.com.

Executing Your Three Big Moves

Once you know your Big Moves, the next challenge is, How do you rally your team to expertly and relentlessly execute them? Even the most clever strategy is worthless without great execution.

Turning your strategic plan into actual growth requires systems, accountability, and persistence. Your team needs to understand not just what your Big Moves are but how to make them happen as well. This is where my team and I spend the majority of our time supporting clients, and it's a topic so enormous it could fill its own book.

While I can't do justice to the topic in this short space, I can tell you that resources from the book *Blue Ocean Strategy* and the One Page Strategic Plan from *Scaling Up* are invaluable.

> **Turning your strategic plan into actual growth requires systems, accountability, and persistence.**

Words of Caution

As we've established, your Big Moves consume massive resources—time, energy, money. I cannot emphasize enough how serious and important your choices are. It's easy to get swept up in the excitement and choose the wrong moves. Let me share two big risks to watch out for.

First, be wary of major technology projects, like ERP or CRM implementations. More often than not, they are giant distractions that cost twice as much and take twice as long as projected. Rarely do they deliver the ROI you expect. These projects may be necessary infrastructure investments, but they aren't your Big Moves. Unless, of course, they make it dramatically easier for customers to do business with you, hand you a clear strategic advantage, or address an existential threat to your business.

Second, watch out for geographic expansion and new lines of business. These are like asking championship golfers to play football. Different games, different rules, different skills. Even incredibly smart leaders can trip up with ventures like this— just like Prishna from chapter 4, the fashion designer who made a flawed attempt to enter the US market.

Your current success can blind you to massive gaps in knowledge, capabilities, and connections. What works brilliantly in your existing market may lead to disaster elsewhere.

This isn't a warning never to expand. It's a reminder to go in with eyes wide open, knowing you're building a new business, not just extending your current one.

In a Nutshell

While improvisation and flexibility can serve a small company well, enduring growth requires a simple, focused approach to strategy. To stay oriented toward the Growth Quadrant:

- Align everyone to a clear vision and a strategy with Three Big Moves to double your company's size in about three years.
- Remember, creating a simple strategy is far more challenging than making a complex one. Expect to put in considerable time and effort to get the ROI.
- It's essential to channel everyone's creativity and resources in the same direction.

Questions

If you already have Three Big Moves for your company:

- *Are they really big enough to match your growth aspirations?*

  _____

  _____

  _____

- *Is there enough focus directly in the Growth Quadrant?*

  _____

  _____

  _____

- *Is your executive team aligned and executing them relentlessly?*

  _____

  _____

  _____

If you don't have Three Big Moves, what could they be?

_____

_____

_____

_____

_____

_____

_____

_____

CHAPTER 11

The Neurosis of Numbers

The temptation to form premature
theories upon insufficient data is
the bane of our profession.

—Sherlock Holmes

Let's say you're about to start your morning run. What's one of
the first things you do? You probably glance at a clock, right?
To calculate how much time you have before your first meeting? Perhaps you check the temperature to ensure you choose
the right gear. Maybe you scan your fitness tracker, noting
your resting heart rate and yesterday's stats.

It can and should be this easy to use numbers to guide your everyday business decisions to stay on the path of growth. But for many reasons, CEOs often lack the numbers they actually need.

I'll tell you about *Rachel, the CEO of an artisanal chocolate business. She prided herself on her incredible gut instinct for business. She told me she could *feel* when a product would be successful. And for a good while, she was right. Her company grew fast, fuelled by a string of hits that seemed to indicate her gut was infallible.

But when I sat down with Rachel last April, her company had just posted its first loss in five years, and she was baffled. "I don't understand," she told me. "Our new product line feels like such a winner. Everyone on the team is so excited about it, so optimistic. But the sales just aren't happening."

Drowning in Data, Thirsting for Insight

As we dug deeper, I could see Rachel was drowning in data— sales figures, customer feedback, market research, consultants' reports. But none of it was telling her why her new chocolates weren't selling or what, if anything, she could do about it.

I see this constantly: empty numbers. Some teams have enormous amounts of data that offer little practical insight for making smarter day-to-day decisions. Others have tons of data they rarely consult. And some teams barely track anything beyond basic accounting.

Rachel had plenty of data but none that led to the insights she needed. She also had plenty of strong opinions from her execs that were not founded in reality. And this is what I call the neurosis of numbers—CEOs and their teams trying to guide a business to growth using lacklustre information.

Your Gut Needs to Be Better Informed

Now, of course, opinion and gut instinct are entirely valid. But there's a fundamental truth that cannot be ignored: Business is a numbers game. You need good numbers to give you a clear picture of reality, and then you can use smarts, gut instincts, and feelings to take you from there.

> Without data, you're just another person with an opinion.
>
> *–W. Edwards Deming*

Guided by Data

Let's go back to the comparison of aviation for a moment. Many CEOs run their companies like pilots who rely entirely on visual cues—navigating based on what they see out the cockpit window, trusting their eyes and instincts to guide them. In the aviation world, these are called *visual-rated pilots*.

This works when a company is relatively small and simple and conditions are perfect. But what happens when visibility drops or unexpected turbulence hits? What happens when a business grows and gets complicated? This is when you need to become the business equivalent of an *instrument-rated pilot*.

Instrument-rated pilots command passenger jets and military aircraft. They are trained to rely on flight instruments instead of eyesight alone, allowing them to navigate safely even when they can't see the horizon. They fly through storms, darkness, and challenging conditions that would ground their visual-only counterparts.

To keep your company growing long term, you need to

become an instrument-rated CEO, your executives need to be instrument-rated leaders, and ultimately, you should aim for an instrument-rated culture across your whole organization.

This means instead of relying solely on gut feelings, personal observations, or surface-level data, you use metrics that give you a precise picture of what's happening in any aspect of your business at any given time.

> **To keep your company growing long term, you need to become an instrument-rated CEO.**

Sixty-Second Insights

To be an instrument-rated leader, you need Sixty-Second Insights.

Sixty-Second Insights are numbers so clear and powerful that you can make smart decisions in less time than it takes to read this section. Just as a pilot can quickly scan the instrument panel and understand every critical detail of the flight, you can have immediate insight into what's working and what's not in your business, allowing you to make better decisions that guide the company to Real Growth.

Let me give you a couple of examples, starting with Andrew Limouris, the founder and CEO of Medix Staffing Solutions, the healthcare staffing agency I mentioned in the intro.

One day I was deep in conversation with Andrew and his leadership team in Chicago, when one of the execs received a strongly worded demand from their biggest customer.

"They're asking for a rebate based on the volume they do," the executive explained.

The account in question was worth $20 million a year in revenue. Needless to say, all attention in the room turned to this dilemma.

"We can't risk losing them," the VP of sales said immediately, and I noticed Andrew nodding.

"Absolutely," another exec chimed in. "A client that size? We've got to keep them happy."

Then the CFO said, "Before we make any decisions, let's take a look at the numbers. Can we pull up the profitability data for this client?"

Now, Medix is a company with its numbers in order. I've worked with them for years, so they are full-fledged, instrument-rated leaders. Within seconds, we had data that told us despite the impressive volume, this client was actually one of the least profitable on a percentage basis.

Some simple napkin math showed us the rebate would have Medix *losing* hundreds of thousands a year to do business with this customer. The rebate exceeded their profit.

Good numbers talk to you. Actually, they scream.

Within minutes, we'd gone from a knee-jerk "yes" to a data-driven "no." No prolonged debates were needed, no agonizing over potential consequences, just a sound decision based on cold, hard facts.

This is what it looks like to have an instrument-rated culture. You have the right information exactly when you need it. All decision-making is informed by facts first.

In a different company without good data, this same

choice would have been emotional, gut-wrenching, and time-consuming. In Andrew's case, he made a decision in minutes, and we continued on with our strategic planning.

Now let's talk about a company I know that delivers gourmet meal kits to busy families. The business had been growing at an unbelievable rate of 50 percent annually for nearly a decade when growth stalled.

The leaders there called me in to help them with a new growth strategy, and we started with a conversation about why sales were declining. They offered fuzzy reasons, blaming the economy and citing a confusing mix of external factors. But something didn't add up.

"Tell me about your customers," I prodded.

"Oh, customers love us," they assured me. "Our customers are like a tap. When we want more sales, we just turn it on."

Imagine my confusion at their level of certainty about this, when I was there to help them with lagging growth. With my spidey senses on red alert, I asked to see their customer feedback data, and I was given eighty pages of spreadsheets to pore over later that day.

Let me tell you, as I scanned that data, I was stunned. The customers were definitely not a controllable tap of revenue—they were a geyser of frustration. Their comments, screaming off the page, spelled out three major issues: late deliveries, missing ingredients, and complicated recipes.

The answer to why growth was slowing was clear as day: Customers were defecting because their concerns were going unaddressed.

When I returned to visit the team the next day and presented them with my findings, they were mortified. Although the company had rigorously collected customer feedback, the executive team had never seen it. Customers were yelling into a void.

The lesson here? Being instrument-rated isn't only about having good data. It's about making a commitment to use it all the time at an operational and executive level.

To become an instrument-rated CEO running an instrument-rated company, here are a few things you need to do.

Know What Good Numbers Look Like

Good numbers talk to you. Actually, they scream. They alert you to potential problems so you can change course before things get dramatic. They identify opportunities that might otherwise go unnoticed. They quickly show you where your time, energy, and money should be invested and where it shouldn't be so you're not throwing good money after bad.

When every part of your business is tracking a few simple operational numbers, something incredible happens. It's easy for teams to be self-managed, not needing constant oversight to stay on track. Teams recalibrate themselves.

Remember Rachel, who struggled to understand why her new chocolates weren't selling? If her team had been instrument-rated, they would have spotted the warning signs buried in her marketing data long before her company posted a loss. They would have ditched the marketing channels that were under-performing and jumped on those showing promise.

> **The goal isn't to amass more data for the sake of it. It's to distill a vast sea of information into meaningful metrics that guide better daily, weekly, and monthly decisions.**

Start with Good Questions

The journey to becoming an instrument-rated leader begins not with answers, but questions.

Too often, leaders find themselves relying on financial dashboards and metrics designed by well-intended tech or finance teams who may not grasp the nuances that drive success or failure at the operational level of each business unit.

Instead, I suggest you ask the people at operational levels across the company what numbers are actually meaningful. What metrics would provide early warning signs of success or failure for specific initiatives? What data would help identify intriguing opportunities or mission-critical problems? Which information would be most valuable for making quick, informed decisions?

If you've got the right data, when quandaries or issues arise, it's easy to do a little bit of napkin math to gut-check almost any situation. Later, you can do more thorough investigating and calculating to confirm your suspicions.

Remember, the goal isn't to amass more data for the sake of it. It's to distill a vast sea of information into meaningful metrics that guide better daily, weekly, and monthly decisions.

Track the Right Numbers

Ultimately, you're aiming to transform your team from Growth Theorists to Growth Scientists. This means learning from both successes and failures to refine your approach over time. To do so, you need two kinds of data on your path to Real Growth:

- **Numbers that guide today's performance:**
  These are your operational numbers. They provide teams across every level of your company with

clear metrics to quickly assess their performance and self-manage. This includes all your business units, departments, the CEO, executives, and the board. These numbers allow for constant calibration of short-term performance, ensuring everyone is aligned, meeting expectations, and optimizing results.

- **Numbers that create future growth:** These are your strategic numbers. They help you see what's working and what's not, related to your long-term strategy, enabling you to recalibrate as needed. They track progress on your Big Moves. They show you how every investment and project is performing against expectations based on ROI. Just as operational numbers let you fine-tune day-to-day operations, strategic numbers allow you to adjust to meet long-term goals.

> ## There's a fundamental truth that cannot be ignored: Business is a numbers game.

Use Your Numbers Like a Smartwatch for Your Business

Think of your operational and strategic numbers like a smartwatch for your business. Just as you might glance at your smartwatch to check your pace on a run, consulting these numbers lets you quickly gauge your performance and calibrate as needed.

By tracking these metrics consistently, you create an instrument-rated culture where decisions are driven by ROI or, for more capital-intensive companies, return on invested capital (ROIC).

Use Your Monthly Meetings to Evaluate and Recalibrate

As a CEO, your monthly business review with your executive team is the golden opportunity to dive deeply into the previous month's performance. I'm not talking about a cursory glance at spreadsheets but a line-by-line examination of what went well and what needs improvement across the company. These meetings are your chance to lead decisively, create sharp focus, and generate performance-based tension that drives the outcomes you're seeking. It's like a hockey team reviewing game tape after a win or a loss.

In these reviews, your leaders are responsible for analyzing every aspect of their business unit, presenting insights—about the good and the bad—and proposing solutions. They should provide updates on your Three Big Moves, review financial performance and operational metrics, and provide insights and actions for their top and bottom talent.

Make this meeting a non-negotiable part of your leadership routine. It's your job to ensure it happens without fail, ask tough questions, highlight areas for improvement, and celebrate wins. In doing this, you're training your leaders to self-manage.

In a Nutshell

The key to staying oriented toward the Growth Quadrant is making swift, smart decisions rather than getting lost in analysis paralysis or relying mostly on gut instinct.

- Like instrument-rated pilots who handle rough weather, you need clear data that helps you make fast, smart decisions as you navigate the complexity of growth.
- Instrument-rated leaders rapidly assess situations based on hard data, allocate resources effectively, and keep the company oriented toward Real Growth.

Questions

Do you and your executives have data at your finger-tips that quickly tells you what's working and what's not for the business?

_____

_____

_____

_____

_____

_____

_____

Where is your data most insightful?

_____

_____

_____

_____

_____

_____

_____

Where is the biggest gap in your data?

_____

_____

_____

_____

_____

_____

PARTING WORDS

The journey is the award.

—Steve Jobs

We've now come to the end of this story about growth, but for you, I hope it marks a beginning.

Throughout these pages, I've shared the best tools and advice I can offer about how to keep a company growing. I hope it may serve as a reference point as you lead your company to its next stage. If any insights from this book help you on your journey, I'll consider this work deeply worthwhile.

As I mentioned at the outset, building a business that sustains growth year after year ranks among life's most formidable challenges. I also believe it's among the most rewarding.

When I think of the deeper rewards, I think of my friend, the late Larry Fisher, who reminded me to use business to serve a higher purpose. When I met Larry in his late seventies, he exemplified how I want to live: thriving in business while embracing life fully. Even in his eighties, he skied more than forty days a year at Whistler.

What struck everyone who knew Larry wasn't his obvious business success—it was his boundless enthusiasm for work and life, an energy that outpaced the energy of leaders half his age. His presence elevated everyone around him with spirited debates and laughter. Until months before his passing, he continued to lead the Lark Group, the construction and development company he built over five decades and which his son Kirk still runs today.

I remember when I taught the *Your Oxygen Mask First* principles to his team, Larry sat in the front row taking more notes than anyone else. At every strategic planning session no matter where we were—his boardroom, a retreat centre, or a hotel—he'd wheel in a cooler of refreshments at 4:00 p.m. to energize the group.

His signature move still makes me smile: He'd pound the boardroom table with childlike excitement, exclaiming, "Profits, profits, profits!" This was always met with an outburst of laughter from the room because everyone knew Larry didn't care about profits for himself. He wanted to do more for the community. He sincerely lived his company's purpose: "To boldly elevate people."

> **True growth transcends profit and loss statements. Growing a business is an opportunity to create waves of positive change throughout your organization, your community, and the world.**

Larry, Kirk, and their executive team built numerous buildings in Metro Vancouver, including in the health and technology district near Surrey Memorial Hospital. Deeply invested in the community, Larry was determined to make Surrey a better place to live and work.

Larry's example reminds me that true growth transcends profit and loss statements. Growing a business is an opportunity to create waves of positive change throughout your organization, your community, and the world. It's an opportunity to witness those around you emerge as stronger people and stronger leaders.

But perhaps the most remarkable gift lies in how this journey transforms you. As you stretch beyond familiar boundaries and tackle increasingly complex challenges, you'll uncover capabilities you didn't even know you had. You'll discover wiser, braver, bolder versions of yourself.

Life is brief, and the path ahead holds no guarantees. But I believe that's precisely why building something meaningful—something that creates value, transforms lives, and leaves a lasting impact—is worth the challenges and heartaches. On your journey of growth, I hope you find the hidden gifts as fulfilling as the victories.

ACKNOWLEDGMENTS

To the countless CEOs, executives, and their teams who invited me behind the scenes on their journeys to growth, thank you for your trust and partnership. Your experiences and insights form the foundation of this book.

In particular, I'd like to thank a few CEOs who directly influenced the thinking in this book, including Obaid Al Tayer, Brent Parent, Angela Santiago, Ben Godsey, Tina Lee, the Gupta brothers (Vishal, Ankur, and Varun), Kirk and Larry Fisher, The LeBlancs (Jean-Pierre, Kate, Kiara, and Phoebe), John McLean, Khalid Al Tayer, Mark Loeppky, Andrew Limouris, and Amish Shah.

To my very first client ever, Steve Majewski, thank you.

Thanks also to Jeff Kaney and Kim "KC" Campbell, who shared their insights and expertise on aviation to bring my flight metaphor to life.

Jim Collins

I'm deeply grateful to Jim Collins, an inspirational human being. His groundbreaking work provides many of the core principles that my team and I use to guide companies toward greatness.

Mentors and Teachers

For some lucky reason, I've had brilliant people mentoring me at every stage of my career. I constantly reflect on their wisdom.

I'm grateful to my first official mentor, Joff Grohne, who modelled how to ask great questions. Other teachers and mentors include Warren Morgan, Thomas Leonard, Greg Clowminzer, Ron Huntington, Richard Aldersea, and Nan O'Connor.

I also have the joy of great collaborators, like Brad Giles, Karen Beattie, Hazel Jackson, and Ed Capaldi for whom I am so thankful.

The Lawrence & Co Team

To the amazing team I get to work with every day at Lawrence & Co, I thank you all. We've built something far beyond what I could have created alone. Our discussions and learning labs contributed to the ideas in this book, and they advance our work with clients.

A special thank you to Kurtis Osborne, COO of Lawrence & Co, who collaborated on the most challenging aspects of this book, offering feedback and clear thinking. Whenever I got stuck, he helped me find simplicity. His partnership in day-to-day operations gave me the time to bring this book to life.

To Janice Watkins, my right hand for almost a quarter of a century—an unimaginable feat!—who manages a million moving pieces, allowing me to focus on what matters most.

Next, I want to give a special acknowledgment to Dean Ritchey, who was the first advisor to join my team. Dean opened my eyes to new possibilities—encouraging me to build a team of advisors when I never intended to do so. In many ways, I see him as the chairman of Lawrence & Co, a trusted voice of wisdom. Through his belief, support, and straight-shooting advice, Dean has been a massive catalyst in shaping Lawrence & Co, now a boutique firm serving leaders around the world.

Book Collaborators

I'm grateful to Amy Humble, whose relentless focus on simplicity challenged me to make this book far clearer and more straightforward than I had first imagined.

And, to Jacqueline Voci, my writing and thought partner on this book. We devoted hundreds of hours to refining and simplifying these ideas. There were many early mornings, weekend meetings, and too many rewrites to count. She helped shape this book into exactly what it needed to be, nothing more and nothing less. It's hilarious that we thought this would be easier to write than *Your Oxygen Mask First*! Thank you for your relentless push for clarity and your willingness to restructure and rethink until we got it right.

To Those Closest to Me

Thank you to my parents, Norm and Lois, who first planted in me the seed of entrepreneurship. To my children, Brayden and Ashley, who are now remarkable adults in their own right, thank you for the joy you bring to me and for your unwavering support. To my extended family and friends, who enrich my life in countless ways. And to Heidi, my partner in life, who inspires me to live life fully and to keep learning and growing.

RESOURCES

Weekly Insights

If this book speaks to you, please sign up for weekly insights via my newsletter. It's tailor-made for CEOs and executives like you: https://lawrenceandco.com/contact. You can also email me at kevin@lawrenceandco.com

The Lawrence & Co Website

You'll find hundreds of resources, including articles, podcasts, and assessments, at the Lawrence & Co website: lawrenceandco.com

4 Forces of Growth

You'll find a curated set of helpful resources specifically related to the 4 Forces of Growth book at: 4forcesofgrowth.com These resources include:

The 4 Forces of Growth Assessments

- CEO assessment
- Team assessment

Article Topics

- Being a strategic CEO
- Building an A-player team
- Strategic planning and execution
- Insightful data
- Profitability

To Share with Your Teams

- Book summary PDF
- Video overviews:
    - Five minutes: The 4 Forces of Growth—In a Nutshell
    - Thirty Minutes: The 4 Forces of Growth— The Video Story
- PowerPoint overview and core images
- Discussion tools

For More Help

If you'd like more direct help, please reach out. Lawrence & Co helps CEOs and executive teams to achieve long-term growth, guiding companies from tens of millions in revenue to hundreds of millions and beyond.

To learn more about working together, visit lawrenceandco .com or send an email to: kevin@lawrenceandco.com